Timeline of Classics

Historical Context for the Good and Great Books

Teacher's Manual

by Gail Ledbetter

Second Edition, February 2016
Institute for Excellence in Writing, L.L.C.

The purchaser of this book receives access to the following downloads:
***Timeline of Classics* e-book, *Sample Vocabulary Cards,* and *Reader Response Journaling Sample Blackline Masters,* as well as articles and talks by Andrew Pudewa and other educators.**

Go to IEW.com/TLC-downloads
(See the blue page for complete download instructions.)

ISBN 978-1-62341-245-6

Institute for Excellence in Writing (IEW®)
8799 N. 387 Rd.
Locust Grove, OK 74352
800.856.5815
info@IEW.com
IEW.com

Printed in the United States of America

Accessing Your Downloads

The purchase of this book entitles its owner to a free download of the following:

- *Timeline of Classics* e-book (121 pages)
- *Reader Response Journaling Sample Blackline Masters* e-book
- *Sample Vocabulary Cards* (3 pages)
- Three pertinent articles by Andrew Pudewa (8 pages)
- Talks by Adam Andrews, Andrew Kern, or Andrew Pudewa (5 MP3s)

To download your e-books, please follow the directions below:

1. Go to our website, IEW.com
2. Sign in to your online customer account. If you do not have an account, you will need to create one.
3. After you are logged in, go to this web page: IEW.com/TLC-downloads
4. Click on the red download arrow.
5. You will be taken to your File Downloads page. Click on the file name, and the e-book or article will download onto your computer.

To download the above-mentioned articles and MP3s, after you are logged in, go to this web page: IEW.com/tlc-info

Please note: You are free to download the MP3s and print these e-books as many times as needed for use within your immediate family or classroom. However, the files are proprietary, and we are trusting you to be on your honor not to share them with anyone. Please see the copyright page for further details. Thank you.

If you have any difficulty receiving these downloads after going through the steps above, please call 800.856.5815.

Institute for Excellence in Writing

8799 N. 387 Road

Locust Grove, OK 74352

Contents

On the Contents page, a given page number indicates a *first* page on which the general historical era is addressed. Every attempt has been made to list literature, a film, or a recording within its historical era. Students of history realize that sometimes the delineations of history into named eras are approximate, may overlap, and may vary, depending on the authority consulted. For example, the years 1780–1830 could be named *Industrialization* or *Urbanization*.

Introduction

What is this resource?

Timeline of Classics: Historical Context for the Good and Great Books reveals a panoramic view of world history. Chronologically indexed, these selected writings, biographies, plays, recordings, and films portray a history of mankind. Please note that while great care was taken in choosing the best of the best, parents and teachers should always *preview or listen in advance to resources*, especially video and audio materials. Created in a simple spreadsheet format, the columns of this resource present

- description/time period
- title of resource
- author
- approximate age/ability level

The timeline is divided into the following broad divisions of world history:

- Ancients
- The Middle Ages
- Renaissance and Reformation
- The Modern World

How is it useful?

One mom summed it up this way: "You could actually organize all of your history and literature studies from elementary through high school using *Timeline of Classics* as your single guide." Browse through the time period you are planning to study, and highlight resources of interest. The book list is completely flexible and offers mere suggestions for age/ability levels to include Elementary (E), Middle (M), and High School (H). By adding the date when a resource has been completed, students will have compiled a complete literature list, which can be recorded on a high school transcript.

For whom is it useful?

Any student or teacher of history and literature can use this portable timeline. For those of us who think chronologically, *Timeline of Classics* provides points of reference for people, places, and events. This versatile reference guide can be used with any teaching style or curriculum. Save hours and hours of planning time and research ... it's already been done for you!

Please visit our website at http://timelineofclassics.com for a detailed description of this one-of-a-kind resource. May *Timeline of Classics* lighten your load as a teacher and strengthen your heart as a student of the Good and Great Books.

Introduction to Reader Response Journaling

In addition to providing a simple reference guide for your study of history through literature, *Timeline of Classics: Historical Context for the Good and Great Books* also provides instruction for teaching students to journal. See page 97 for an example of a Reader Response Journal.

You may be wondering why on earth you would want to teach your students to journal about literature. After all, they did read the book. Isn't that good enough? Often, reading is woefully inadequate. Here's a story to illustrate my point. While taking a group of third grade boys through a beloved children's classic, I learned the priceless value of Socratic discussion and the necessity for vocabulary study. (A mother sometimes assumes that some things in life are obvious to their children. This mother was wrong!) After progressing about halfway through E.B. White's *Charlotte's Web*, it became obvious that no one in my little band of boys knew the meaning of *infant*, though each of them had one living in his home!

There are many ways to read a book. Reading a passage does not automatically ensure comprehension or understanding. Investing the time and effort to develop essential thinking skills in students of all ages is crucial. Training students to journal through literature is a powerful method for accomplishing many key thinking skills. After considering with me some of the goals, outcomes, and process of journaling, perhaps you will agree that it is a worthy task.

The Goals of Journaling about Literature

Although the *goals* of journaling about literature could become vast and numerous, I will point out a few that I have observed. Discussion, vocabulary study, and journaling slow down the brain and allow students to think more deeply about literature. The practice of keyword outlining not only strengthens comprehension but enables students to recall complex details with ease. Elaborate plots and multiple characters no longer create confusion. Readers become much more attentive to literary devices, enabling them to make their own writing come alive. Purposefully done, journaling about literature disciplines the mind.

The Anticipated Outcomes of Journaling through a Book

Those who practice journaling through literature with their students can anticipate a variety of *outcomes*. You will enjoy it! Forging memories with your students is priceless. As you take the time to allow literature to do its work, your soul will be enriched. Cumulatively you and your older students will amass a storehouse of quotations and passages, which can be alluded to in future essay writing. Classic masterpieces provide something to imitate while writing. You will remember what you write about! Before you know it, you and your students will have expanded your ever-increasing vocabulary. Teachers will enjoy a meaningful way of measuring true student comprehension. Older students will benefit from having been trained to think as they approach writing assignments in high school, college, and beyond. Grounding your students in attentiveness to detail will sharpen future debate skills. You will have discussed a book so thoroughly with your students that they will be armed and dangerous—that's right! Your more advanced writers will have seen how to create a thesis statement, accumulate valid arguments, and construct a complete persuasive essay. The results of your labor will speak for themselves.

Are you convinced yet? Now that I have given you a daunting assignment, let me reassure you. The methods for journaling suggested here may seem complicated and difficult, but they are not. You can do this! Let me show you how.

The Process of Journaling about Literature

May I begin by saying that I am a mom like many of you. When I began working on *Timeline of Classics*, my children spanned in age from toddler to high school student with two in between. During my career as a mom, we laughed and cried our way through countless classics. During my career as a teacher, we learned a few useful tactics along the way. Over time I discovered that what we did naturally with a stack of beloved classics, a composition book, and a few stuffed animals fostered a lifetime love of books in my children and me. I had no idea that the simple reader response journals we kept when my kids were young would provide a springboard for more advanced assignments. Many years later I discovered that this type of journal was common among teachers of literary analysis. IEW author Lesha Myers referred to this as a dialectical journal. Prepare yourself for success! This will require time, patience, and perseverance, but the end result will yield countless blessings to you and your students. So, how do you begin the *process* of learning and teaching literature?

• Step 1- Teach an introduction to literature.

Teaching the Classics: A Socratic Method for Literary Education by Adam and Missy Andrews was designed to make classic literature accessible to everyone. In their course they utilize children's literature to illustrate the elements of fiction (context, structure, and style) which are common to all literature. Socratic-style discussion questions, along with concepts modeled from children's literature, make the task of literary analysis very doable. Their course includes modified versions of *Peter Rabbit*, "Paul Revere's Ride," "Rikki-Tikki-Tavi," *Tom Sawyer*, *Martin the Cobbler*, and *Huckleberry Finn*. What better way to learn literary devices? Children's literature is the ticket! *Teaching the Classics* is my go-to seminar. This program, or something comparable, is essential in order to prepare you for beginning literary analysis.

• Step 2- Begin with simple stories and fairy tales.

After learning the basics from *Teaching the Classics*, choose your own fable or fairy tale to discuss. Remember, this approach takes practice, so start small. Here are a few quality resources for finding good stories to discuss: Aesop's Fables, Grimms' Fairy Tales, *The Annotated Hans Christian Andersen* by Maria Tatar, and *The Book of Virtues* and *The Moral Compass* by William J. Bennett.

• Step 3- Organize your thoughts.

Keep in mind that thinking is messy! Provide your students with a place to organize their thoughts as they practice Socratic discussion, learn to think, discover literary devices, and more.

In addition to utilizing the Andrews' story chart found in *Teaching the Classics*, now is the perfect time to brush up on your IEW note-making and outlining skills! Andrew Pudewa teaches you how in IEW Units 1 and 2 of *Teaching Writing: Structure and Style*. Revisit IEW Unit 3: Retelling Narrative Stories to learn a quick and efficient method for teaching your students and yourself how to analyze a story or book.

Teach your students to construct a key word outline while asking and answering questions related to narrative stories. I normally work up both types of charts with my classes. (A link for sample outlines is provided in this resource. See the blue page.) Practice this type of outlining with a few classic favorites such as "The Musicians of Bremen," "Hansel and Grethel," "Rapunzel," "Cinderella," "Little Red Riding Hood," "The Fisherman and His Wife," "Rumpelstiltskin," "Snow White and the Seven Dwarfs," "The Ugly Duckling," "The Princess and the Pea," "The Steadfast Tin Soldier," or "The Little Mermaid." As you can see, the list of possibilities is nearly endless! (Please note that original classic fairy tales are much different than the Disney versions.)

• Step 4- *Then* move on to a book.

I prefer getting to know my students before making our book selection together. We read only the unabridged version of a book. Choosing titles that are old enough to be in the public domain almost always ensures that there is an audio version of the book.

Allowing students the option of listening to the book while they read offers a variety of benefits. It dramatically reduces the problem of mispronunciation. It easily provides expression and nuances by the narrator that help to paint the author's picture in the reader's mind. It allows students who are weaker readers to enjoy the book and keep up with the class when they may not otherwise be able to do so.

In a group setting be sure that everyone is reading from the same edition of the book. You will create a train wreck for yourself if students are allowed to read from different versions.

Note: Please work through *Teaching the Classics* or another introduction to literary analysis before tackling a book.

Ideas for Vocabulary Study

Do not neglect the study of vocabulary. Classic literature is filled with challenging words! Here is one effective way of engaging students to expand their working vocabulary:

1. Write the **vocabulary word** on the unlined side of an index card. (I prefer 4" x 6" cards, but use whatever you like.) Write the **chapter number** in the lower right-hand corner.
2. Divide the lined side of the card into four equal rectangular sections.
3. In the upper left-hand corner, give the appropriate **definition** of the word; name **synonyms** or **antonyms** as appropriate.
4. In the lower left-hand corner, use the vocabulary word in a **complete sentence**.
5. In the upper right-hand corner, tell the appropriate **part of speech** which matches the context from the story.
6. In the lower right-hand corner, draw a simple **picture** to illustrate the word.
7. Use these vocabulary cards however you like: for playing games or for beefing up writing assignments.

Sample vocabulary cards, a completed reader response journal for *The Magician's Nephew*, articles, and MP3s are available to you at IEW.com/TLC-downloads (see the blue page).

> This is the great power of literature, that by its power our parents long dead can speak to us, and we can listen to them. And if they do not seem to answer when we ask, it may be only because we have not turned the page. And this is the great value of a thoughtful parent or any other true teacher in any other guise—that he has turned many pages. - Richard Mitchell, *The Gift of Fire*

May you turn many pages!

Gail Ledbetter

Materials Needed

The pages of this resource contain information students and their families will use for years of studying memorable literature, plays, and films. Should a website's link not work when you search online, however, go to this webpage: IEW.com/tlc-info

The purchaser of this book may access additional Reader Response Journals here: IEW.com/TLC-downloads (See the blue page for complete download instructions.)

Ancients

Timeline of Classics

Description or Time Period	Title	Author	Level
flow of history from 5000 BC to modern times in a table format that includes history and politics, literature and theater, religion and philosophy, visual arts and music, science and technology, and daily life	*The Timetables of History: A Horizontal Linkage of People and Events* (directly translated from *Kulturfahrplan: The Culture Timetables*)	Bernard Grun (based on the work of Werner Stein and Wallace Brockway)	E M H
spiral-bound book of card stock printed with a blank timeline; perfect for stickers, drawings, annotations, etc. for tracing the relations between events, people, ideas, discoveries, civilizations, and kingdoms	*Book of Time: Blank time line from 5000 BC to the present*	InquisiCorp Corporation http://sonlight.com	E M H
from earliest times to the present; a large, detailed colorful fold-out resource	*The Wall Chart of World History*	Barnes & Noble, Inc.	E M H
early civilizations, c. 8000–900 BC	*World History Atlas*	http://maps.com	E M H
Western civilization from prehistoric man through the modern nation-state; as told by a grandfather to his grandchildren	*The Story of Mankind*	Hendrik Willem van Loon (updated by Gerrit van Loon and John M. Merriman)	E M
Western civilization from prehistoric man through the modern nation-state; as told by a grandfather to his grandchildren	*The Story of Mankind* (based on the book by Hendrik Willem van Loon)	1957 film adaptation starring the Marx Brothers and Ronald Colman	H
literature of Western culture through the Renaissance	*The Norton Anthology of World Masterpieces Volume 1*	Maynard Mack, general editor	H
fifty volumes of selected world classics from all main divisions of literature	*Fifteen Minutes a Day Reading Guide for The Harvard Classics (1909)*	Charles W. Eliot, editor of *The Harvard Classics*	H
Scriptures arranged chronologically	*The Daily Bible*	F. LaGard Smith	E M H
the *big picture* for understanding the Old Testament	*Putting Together the Puzzle of the Old Testament*	Bill Jones	M H
Chronological Bible; comic book form	*Good and Evil*	Michael Pearl	E M H
Creation to 433 BC	*What the Bible is All About for Young Explorers*	Frances Blankenbaker	E M
helping children defend their faith	*The Seven C's of History*	Stacia McKeever	E M
Creation to Reformation; the New World	*Streams of Civilization (Volume One)*	Mary Stanton and Albert Hyma	E M
10,000 BC–present	*The Kingfisher Atlas of World History: A Pictorial Guide to the World's People and Events*	Simon Adams	E M H

There are 850,000 volumes in the Imperial Library at Paris. If a man were to read industriously from dawn to dark for sixty years, he would die in the first alcove. Would that some charitable soul, after losing a great deal of time among the false books and alighting upon a few true ones, which made him happy and wise, would name those which have been bridges or ships to carry him safely over dark morasses and barren oceans, into the heart of sacred cities, into palaces and temples.

—Ralph Waldo Emerson

Description or Time Period	Title	Author	Level
world history for children	*Kingfisher History Encyclopedia*	edited by Charlotte Evans	E M H
historical atlas	*The Kingfisher Atlas of the Ancient World*	Simon Adams	E M
Creation; evolution; Genesis	*The Answers Book*	Ken Ham et al.	H
the gospel from Genesis	*A is for Adam*	Ken and Mally Ham	E
Creation science	*Amazing Story of Creation from Science and the Bible*	Duane T. Gish	E M
historical consequences and impact	*The Bible and Ancient Thought Part 1 (World Views of the Western World)*	David Quine http://cornerstonecurriculum.com	H
from the earliest nomads to the last Roman Emperor	*The Story of the World/Volume 1: Ancient Times*	Susan Wise Bauer http://peacehillpress.com	E M
from the earliest nomads to the last Roman Emperor	*The Story of the World/Volume 1: Ancient Times*	unabridged reading by Jim Weiss http://greathall.com	E M
matching history with the Bible	*World History Made Simple*	Ruth Beechick	H
presenting a biblical world view	*Answers Magazine*	Answers in Genesis http://AnswersMagazine.com	E M H
Abraham through to present day	*The Kingdom Strikes Back*	John Holzmann	E M
collection of stories, poems, and essays	*The Book of Virtues: A Treasury of Great Moral Stories*	William J. Bennett	E M H
people of great character from early mythology to modern times	*The Children's Book of Heroes*	edited by William J. Bennett illustrated by Michael Hague	E
overview of history	*A Child's History of the World*	Virgil M. Hillyer	E
complete and comprehensive text	*Western Civilization*	Jackson J. Spielvogel	M H
reference guide; understanding our culture through great Western literary classics	*Invitation to the Classics: A Guide to Books You've Always Wanted to Read*	Louise Cowan and Os Guinness, editors	M H
timeline	*History Through the Ages*	Amy Pak	E
condensed description of each era	*Pocket History*	Philip Steele	M H
prehistory to Post-Modern era	*The Annotated Mona Lisa: A Crash Course in Art History From Prehistoric to Post-Modern*	Carol Strickland	M H
selections from around the world	*Favorite Poems Old and New*	Helen Ferris	E M H

The *Bible* forms the lowest stratum in the teaching of literature. It should be taught so early and so thoroughly that it sinks straight to the bottom of the mind, where everything that comes along later can settle on it.

—Northrup Frye

Description or Time Period	Title	Author	Level
creation to Egypt—history, literature, linguistics, art, geography, and theology	*Genesis: Finding Our Roots*	Ruth Beechick http://mottmedia.com	H
from creation to Abram; linguistics, archaeology, astronomy, etc.	*Adam and His Kin*	Ruth Beechick http://mottmedia.com	E M H
Ancient Egypt; Biblical history	*Joseph*	Brian Wildsmith	E
1st-place winner at Vision Forum's 2004 Independent Christian Film Festival	*Biology 101: Biology According to the Days of Creation*	Wes Olson	M H
Ancient Egypt	*Mummies, Tombs, and Treasure: Secrets of Ancient Egypt*	Lila Perl	E
Ancient Egypt—biographical dictionary with color pictures, charts, and timelines	*The Ancient Egyptians*	Lila Perl	E
Ancient Egypt	*Egypt*	Stephen Krensky	E
Ancients and Medieval to the present	*The Picture History of Great Inventors*	Gillian Clements	E M H
Great Pyramid at Giza by Khufu	*The Great Pyramid*	Elizabeth Mann	E
how mummies were buried and preserved	*Mummies Made in Egypt*	Aliki	E
Ancient Egypt—mummification	*See-Through Mummies*	John Malam	E
Ancient Egyptian pharaoh; successful and powerful female ruler: Hatshepsut	*Lost Queen of Egypt*	Lucile Morrison	M H
explore Egyptian art through Tut's tomb; the Shrines at Thebes, etc.	*Ancient Egyptian Design*	Ed Sibbett, Jr.	E
Egyptian tomb decorations to modern art	*Usborne Introduction to Art*	Rosie Dickins	E M H
Ancient Egypt, Rome, Medieval Europe, and Viking days	*The Usborne Time Traveler*	Usborne http://usbornebooks.com	E
how differing languages and races occurred	*Tower of Babel*	Jon Taylor, illustrator	E
how people are different; languages, money, food, clothing, religions, etc.	*Around the World Series* (reprint of Usborne classics)	Carol Bowyer	E M
chronology of Ancient Egypt	*Pharaohs of Ancient Egypt*	Elizabeth Payne	E M
3000 BC—Ancient Egypt	*Egyptian Treasures: Mummies and Myths* (audio storytelling recording)	Jim Weiss http://greathall.com	E M

And Isaiah said: "He'll bear no beauty or glory. Rejected, despised, a man of such sorrow, we'll cover our eyes. He'll take up our sickness and carry our tears, and for his people he will be pierced. He'll be crushed for our evils, our punishment feel, and by his wounds we will be healed." From you, O Bethlehem, small among Judah, a ruler will come, ancient and strong.

—Andrew Peterson, *Behold the Lamb of God*

Description or Time Period	Title	Author	Level
3000 BC—China	*Tales from Cultures Far and Near* (audio storytelling recording)	Jim Weiss http://greathall.com	E M
Ancient Egypt	*Boy of the Pyramids: A Mystery of Ancient Egypt*	Ruth Fosdick Jones	E M
Ancient Egypt	*Growing Up in Ancient Egypt*	Rosalie David	E
Ancient Egypt	*Motel of the Mysteries*	David Macaulay	E
Egyptian Myths	*The Gods and Goddesses of Ancient Egypt*	Leonard Everett Fisher	E
myths and legends of the world	*The Crystal Pool*	Geraldine McCaughrean	E
c. 2700 BC	*The Epic of Gilgamesh*	Anonymous poet; Geraldine McCaughrean	E M H
Mesopotamia; clay tablets; pagan legends	*Gilgamesh Trilogy*	Ludmila Zeman	E
ancient pagan view of creation	*Gilgamesh*	David Ferry	M
Ancient Egypt	*The Mystery of the Hieroglyphs*	Carol Donoughue	E
2350 BC—size of ark, care of animals, etc.	*In the Days of Noah*	Earl and Bonnie Snellenberger	M
2350 BC	*The True Story of Noah's Ark*	Tom Dooley	E M
2250–1800 BC—Ancient Egypt	*Shipwrecked Sailor*	John Foster	E
2200 BC—Ancient Egypt	*Pyramid*	David Macaulay	E M H
1915–1406 BC—Joseph to Joshua	*The Golden Goblet*	Eloise Jarvis McGraw	E M
1900–1700 BC—Judaism; Abraham	*One World, Many Religions*	Mary Pope Osborne	E M
1792 BC	*Codes of Hammurabi and Moses*	W. W. Davies	M H
c. 1446–c. 6/5 BC—musical presentation of God's deliverance of the Hebrew people	*Behold the Lamb of God*	Andrew Peterson http://andrew-peterson.com/behold	E M H
1446 BC—Hebrew slavery; Egypt; Exodus	*Tirzah*	Lucille Travis	E
1406–433 BC; Judges to Malachi	*D'Aulaire's Book of Greek Myths*	Ingri and Edgar Parin D'Aulaire	E
1343 BC—Egyptian Pharaoh's tomb	*Tut's Mummy Lost and Found*	Judy Donnelly	E
historical fiction written on papyrus	*Tutankhamen's Gift*	Robert Sabuda	E
1343 BC—Egypt; narration of the exhibit and tomb of Tutankhamen	*Tut, the Boy King*	narrated by Orson Welles	M H
1250–1240 BC—Troy; epic Greek poem	*The Iliad* (by Homer)	Ian Strachan; Victor Ambrus, illustrator	E M

But Nestor did not let matters rest there. Other thoughts had been preying on his mind, and he could hold them back no longer. "This all started that day, great king, when you infuriated Achilles and took the girl Briseis from his tent. Against our advice, you gave way to your anger and disgraced him before us all by seizing his prize. And you keep her still." Agamemnon, his brow furrowed with worry, nodded. "That's no lie, old man. I was blinded by pride."

–Homer, *The Iliad*, retold by Ian Strachan

Description or Time Period	Title	Author	Level
Troy; Odysseus; translation for young children	*The Children's Homer: The Adventures of Odysseus and The Tale of Troy*	Padraic Colum	E M
journey home following the Trojan War	*Odysseus*	Geraldine McCaughrean	E
introduction to the Trojan War	*The Trojan Horse*	Emily Little	E
Troy	*Black Ships Before Troy: The Story of the Iliad*	Rosemary Sutcliff	E
1250 BC—Carthage, Sicily, and Italy after the Trojan War; destruction of Troy	*The Aeneid* (*Compact Classics: Vol. III*/p. 47)	Virgil	H
Trojan warrior Aeneas	*In Search of a Homeland: The Story of the Aeneid*	Penelope Lively	E
1250 BC—Ancient Egypt	*The Cat of Bubastes: A Story of Ancient Egypt*	George Alfred Henty	M H
1250 BC—Ancient Egypt	*The Cat of Bubastes: A Story of Ancient Egypt* (audio storytelling recording)	adapted and retold by Jim Weiss http://greathall.com	E M H
1250 BC—Ancient Egypt	*The Cat of Bubastes: A Story of Ancient Egypt* (unabridged audio book)	Jim Hodges http://jimhodgesaudiobooks.com	E M H
c. 1250 BC—ancient Phrygian city; NW Asia Minor; Trojan war fought over them	*The Trojan Women* (*Compact Classics: Vol. II*/p. 9)	Euripides	H
Ancient Greece; Corinth	*Medea* (*Compact Classics: Vol. II*/p. 11)	Euripides	H
Ancient Egypt	*Tales of Ancient Egypt*	Roger Lancelyn Green	E M
c. 1240–1230 BC—after the fall of Troy	*Odyssey of Homer*	Barbara Leonie Picard	M H
c. 1240–1230 BC—after the fall of Troy; a retelling of the Odyssey for children	*The Wanderings of Odysseus*	Rosemary Sutcliff	E
c. 1240–1230 BC—Greek islands; ten years after the fall of Troy; Greek literature	*The Odyssey*	Geraldine McCaughrean	E
c. 1250–1240 BC—epic Greek poem; Troy	*The Iliad*	Homer	H
c. 1240–1230 BC—Greek islands; ten years after the fall of Troy; Greek literature	*The Odyssey*	Homer	H
1200 BC—Palestine, Israel; time of the Judges: Deborah, Barak, Jotham, and Uriah	*Hittite Warrior*	Joanne Williamson	E M

Behind both feet he pierced the tendons, heel to ankle. Rawhide cords he drew through both and lashed them to his chariot, letting the man's head trail. Stepping aboard, bearing the great trophy of the arms, he shook the reins, and whipped the team ahead into a willing run. A dust cloud rose above the furrowing body; the dark tresses flowed behind, and the head so princely once lay back in dust.

—Homer, *The Iliad*

Description or Time Period	Title	Author	Level
1200 BC—The Trojan War; last year of the Greek siege of Troy	*The Iliad of Homer* (written in c. 750 BC) (*Compact Classics: Vol. III*/p. 49)	Homer Richmond Lattimore, translator	M H
returning home after the Trojan War; ten years later	*The Odyssey of Homer* (Compact Classics: Vol. III/p. 51)	Homer Richmond Lattimore, translator	M H
background facts and photographs	*DK Classics: The Odyssey by Homer*	Adrian Mitchell illustrated by Stuart Robertson	E M
c. 1200–1100 BC—Sicilian coast	*Cyclops (Compact Classics: Vol. II/p. 7)*	Euripides	H
Greek and Roman mythology	*Mythology*	Edith Hamilton	M H
Ancient Greece and Rome	*The Greek Way*	Edith Hamilton	M H
H Greek and Roman Myths	*The Gods and Goddesses of Olympus*	Aliki	E
Greek gods	*Greek Gods and Goddesses*	Geraldine McCaughrean	E
Greek and Roman Myths—picture book	*Pandora*	Robert Burleigh	E
Greek and Roman Myths	*Twelve Labors of Hercules*	Marc A. Cerasini	E
Greek and Roman Myths	*King Midas: The Golden Touch*	Demi	E
Greek and Roman Myths	*Theseus and the Minotaur*	Leonard Everett Fisher	E
1000 BC—Ancient Greece—Athens	*A Midsummer Night's Dream* (*Compact Classics: Vol. II*/p. 27)	William Shakespeare	H
1000 BC—Ancient Greece—Athens	*A Midsummer Night's Dream* (audio storytelling recording)	adapted and retold by Jim Weiss http://greathall.com	E M
1000 BC—Israel	*A Treasury of Wisdom: Solomon* (audio storytelling recording)	Jim Weiss http://greathall.com	E M
16 read-aloud Greek and Roman Myths	*Greek Myths*	Geraldine McCaughrean	E
1000 BC—Greece	*Heroes in Mythology* (audio storytelling recording)	Jim Weiss http://greathall.com	E M
Greek myth—selfishness and redemption	*Till We Have Faces*	C. S. Lewis	M
874–853 BC—King Ahab; Israel; Old Testament	*Adara*	Beatrice Gormley	E
757–386 BC—from the founding of Rome to the Gallic invasion	*The Early History of Rome*	Livy	H
c. 715 BC—Persia, Israel, and Palestine	*Within the Palace Gates: The King's Cupbearer*	Anna P. Siviter	E M
701 BC—Kushite dynasty; Hezekiah	*God King*	Joanne Williamson	E M

Never, not in their darkest moments, do they (the Greeks) lose their taste for life. It is always a wonder and a delight, the world a place of beauty, and they themselves rejoicing to live in it.

—Edith Hamilton, *The Greek Way*

Description or Time Period	Title	Author	Level
620–560 BC	*Aesop's Fables*	Aesop; Jack Zipes, editor	E M H
Aesop through Renaissance Europe	*Animal Tales* (audio storytelling recording)	Jim Weiss http://greathall.com	E M H
c. 551–479 BC—China	*Confucius: China's Wise Teacher (Compact Classics: Vol. I/*4-E5)	Biography: Leaders of the Spirit	M H
c. 536–530 BC—Nebuchadnezzar; Babylon	*The Handwriting on the Wall: Secrets from the Prophecies of Daniel*	David Jeremiah	H
509 BC—from the fall of Rome to the Atomic Age; analysis of key moments, men, and ideas; influence on the condition and direction of our present culture	*How Should We Then Live: The Rise and Decline of Western Thought and Culture*	Francis A. Schaeffer	H
ancient physicians of pharaoh to modern genetic engineering	*The History of Medicine*	John Hudson Tiner	E
Spartan life; ancient Greek history	*Theras and His Town*	Caroline Dale Snedeker	E
480 BC—the Battle of Thermopylae; told by the only survivor	*The Spartan*	Caroline Dale Snedeker	E
480 BC—Ancient Greece; Spartans vs. Persian army; battle of Thermopylae	*Three Hundred Spartans*	1962 film	M H
480–460 BC—Greek tragedy	*The Bacchae*	Euripides; Phillip Vellacott, translator	H
Ancient Egypt	*The Ten Commandments*	1956 film starring Charlton Heston and Yul Brynner	E M H
469–399 BC—Athens; trial and death of Socrates; Greek moral philosophy	*The Socratic Dialogues of Plato (Compact Classics: Vol. II/p. 371)*	Plato	M H
469–399 BC—Athens; Plato recorded the dialogues of Socrates	*The Last Days of Socrates (469–399 BC)*	Plato Hugh Tredennick, translator	M H
458 BC—trilogy of Greek tragic plays	*The Oresteia (Compact Classics: Vol. II/p. 3)*	Aeschylus	H
Ancient Greece	*Excavating the Past: Ancient Greece*	Christine Hatt	E M
431–404 BC—Greek historian; father of scientific history records the achievements of Greek culture, human nature, and lessons learned from history	*The Landmark Thucydides: A Comprehensive Guide to The Peloponnesian War*	Thucydides Robert B. Strassler, editor	H
c. 430–425 BC—first surviving history of the Greeks and Asiatic peoples	*History of the Persian Wars*	Herodotus	H
rise of the Persian Empire; fall to Greek city-states; Western civilization established	*The Landmark Herodotus: The Histories*	Herodotus (the father of history) Andrea L. Purvis, translator	M H

No man should bring children into the world who is unwilling to persevere to the end in their nurture and education.

—Plato

Description or Time Period	Title	Author	Level
430 BC—the story of Nehemiah	*Within the Palace Gates: The King's Cupbearer*	Anna Pierpont Siviter	E
c. 429–425 BC—classical tragedy; struggle for truth	*Oedipus Rex* (Oedipus the King) (*Compact Classics: Vol. I*/5-M3)	Sophocles I David Grene, translator Richmond Lattimore, editor	M H
Greek tragedies—Oedipus the King; Oedipus at Colonus; Antigone	*Theban Trilogy* (*Compact Classics: Vol. II*/p. 5)	Sophocles David Grene, translator	M H
425–388 BC—witty Greek playwright	*Comedies*	Aristophanes	H
400 BC—Sicily; Archimedes	*Galileo and the Stargazers* (audio storytelling recording)	Jim Weiss http://greathall.com	E M
384–322 BC—Macedonia	*Aristotle "Scientist and Prince of Philosophers"* (*Compact Classics: Vol. I*/4-C5)	Biography: Artists and Philosophers	H
c. 384–322 BC—systematic, logical, and investigative approach to philosophy	*Nichomachean Ethics* (Plato's greatest student) (*Compact Classics: Vol. II*/p. 373)	Aristotle	H
c. 384–322 BC	*Aristotle for Everybody*	Mortimer Adler	H
c. 375 BC—Greek philosophy; defense of wisdom and virtue; highly influential in shaping Western civilization and thought	*The Republic* (*Compact Classics: Vol. I*/5-K5)	Plato Robin Waterfield, translator	H
332 BC—Ancient Egypt	*Mara, Daughter of the Nile*	Eloise Jarvis McGraw	M H
356–323 BC; conqueror of the ancient world and student of Aristotle	*Alexander the Great*	Robert Green	E
356–323 BC—Greece	*Alexander the Great*	John Gunther	E M
356–323 BC—Greece	*Alexander the Great: Conqueror of the Ancient World*	Tom McGowen	M
356–323 BC—Greece	*A Treasury of Wisdom: Alexander the Great* (audio storytelling recording)	Jim Weiss http://greathall.com	E M
336 BC—Athens; Western thought	*Introduction to Aristotle*	Richard McKeon	H
c. 300 BC; library at Alexandria, Egypt; textbook of Geometry: The Elements	*Euclid: "Geometry's Genius"* (*Compact Classics: Vol. I*/4-A1)	Biography: Pioneers in Science	M H
287–212 BC—Syracuse	*Archimedes and the Door of Science*	Jeanne Bendick	E

Men of Athens, I honour and love you; but I shall obey God rather than you, and while I have life and strength I shall never cease from the practice and teaching of philosophy, exhorting any one whom I meet and say ... are you not ashamed of heaping up the greatest amount of money and honour and reputation, and caring so little about wisdom and truth and the greatest improvement of the soul, which you never regard or heed at all?

—Plato

Description or Time Period	Title	Author	Level
275–194 BC—Eratosthenes—Greek scholar, poet, and inventor discovers the circumference of the Earth	*The Librarian Who Measured the Earth*	Kathryn Lasky	E M
264–146 BC—Punic Wars to the destruction of Carthage	*The Rise of the Roman Republic*	Polybius	H
220 BC—Ancient Rome and Carthage, Italy	*The Young Carthaginian: A Story of the Times of Hannibal*	G.A. Henty	M H
220 BC—Ancient Rome and Carthage, Italy; Hannibal's campaign	*The Young Carthaginian: A Story of the Times of Hannibal* (audio storytelling recording)	adapted and retold by Jim Weiss http://greathall.com	E M H
220 BC—Ancient Rome and Carthage, Italy; Hannibal's campaign	*The Young Carthaginian: A Story of the Times of Hannibal* (unabridged audio book)	Jim Hodges http://jimhodgesaudiobooks.com	E M H
218–202 BC—Second Punic War; Carthage; Rome	*The War with Hannibal*	Livy Aubrey De Selincourt, translator	H
200–220 BC—first emperor of China	*The Great Wall of China*	Leonard Everett Fisher	E
196 BC—Rosetta Stone; hieroglyphs—the true story of the translator	*Seeker of Knowledge*	James Rumford	E
196 BC—Rosetta Stone; hieroglyphs	*The Riddle of the Rosetta Stone*	James Cross Giblin	E
106–43 BC—bilingual writer; Greek and Latin; most famous orator of ancient Rome	*Cicero: Selected Works*	Cicero Michael Grant, translator	H
1st century Greek historian: Strabo	*The Egyptian Cinderella*	Shirley Climo	E
biographies of Ancient Romans	*Lives of Famous Romans*	Olivia Coolidge	E
Greece—Rome transition	*A Triumph for Flavius*	Caroline Dale Snedeker	E
Classical Greece and Rome	*The Ancient City: Life in Classical Athens and Rome*	Peter Connolly	M
Ancient Persian sultan; Shahrazad	*Shadow Spinner*	Susan Fletcher	E M
King Ahab; life and times of the Old Testament; set during the time of Second Kings	*Adara*	Beatrice Gormley	E
Ancient Persia	*Hadassah: The Girl Who Became Queen Esther*	Tommy Tenney	E
Ancient Persia; King Xerxes; young Jewish orphan becomes Esther, Queen of Persia	*One Night with the King*	2006 film starring Peter O'Toole and Omar Sharif	H
1st century Ancient Judea and Rome during the time of Jesus Christ	*Ben-Hur: A Tale of the Christ (Compact Classics: Vol. I*/5-E4)	Lew Wallace	H
Ancient Rome; Jewish customs	*Ben-Hur* (based on book by General Lew Wallace)	1959 film starring Charlton Heston	M H
Ancient Rome	*City: A Story of Roman Planning and Construction*	David Macaulay	M

Mathematics reveals its secrets only to those who approach it with pure love, for its own beauty.

—Archimedes

Description or Time Period	Title	Author	Level
Ancient Rome	*Roman Way to Western Civilization*	Edith Hamilton	M H
c. 69 BC—queen of Ancient Egypt	*Cleopatra*	Diane Stanley and Peter Vennema	E
58–51 BC	*Caesar's Gallic Wars*	Olivia Coolidge	E M
54–51 BC—philosophical Socratic-style dialogue on Roman politics	*De re Publica* (On the Commonwealth)	Cicero	H
48 BC—Alexandria, Egypt, and Rome; historic tragedy based on Plutarch's "Life of Marcus Antonius"	*Antony and Cleopatra* *(Compact Classics: Vol. II/p. 21)*	William Shakespeare Roma Gill, editor	H
44 BC—Ancient Rome—tragic drama; assassination	*Julius Caesar (Compact Classics: Vol. I/5-M1)*	William Shakespeare John Andrews, editor	M H
44 BC—Ancient Rome	*Julius Caesar*	1953 film starring Marlon Brando	E M H
44 BC—Rome	*Julius Caesar and the Story of Rome* (audio storytelling recording)	Jim Weiss http://greathall.com	E M H
44 BC—fall of Roman Republic; beginning of the Roman Empire	*Julius Caesar*	Rachel Firth	E
43 BC–AD 18—short stories of Roman society and conduct	*Metamorphosis*	Ovid Charles Martin, translator	H
19 BC—epic of Western Civilization describing intense human experiences	*The Aeneid*	Virgil	H
Italian family life; Latin poetry	*Ecologues and Georgics*	Virgil; James Rhoades, translator	H
AD 1–300—Jesus, Paul, and Early Church	*Augustus Caesar's World*	Genevieve Foster	E M
Biblical world view contrasted with Greek-Roman world view	*World Views of the Western World: The Bible and Ancient Thought* (Part 1)	David Quine http://cornerstonecurriculum.com	H
AD 14–68—reigns of Tiberius through Nero; pagan world of early Christians	*The Annals of Imperial Rome*	Tacitus Michael Grant, translator	H
Ancient Rome; Nero; lions; crucifixion	*Quo Vadis*	Henryk Sienkiewicz	H
Ancient Rome; Nero; lions; crucifixion	*Quo Vadis* (based on the novel by Henryk Sienkiewicz)	1951 film starring Peter Ustinov	H
AD 37–68—reign of Nero; persecution of first-century Christians	*Quintus*	R. Weerstand	E
Ancient Rome—the story of the Gospel	*The Greatest Story Ever Told*	1965 film starring Charlton Heston	M H

Brutus: Grant that, and then is death a benefit. So are we Caesar's friends, that have abridged his time of fearing death. Stoop, Romans, stoop, and let us bathe our hands in Caesar's blood up to the elbows, and besmear our swords. Then walk we forth, even to the market-place, and waving our red weapons o'er our heads, let's all cry "Peace, freedom, and liberty!"

—*Julius Caesar* by William Shakespeare

Description or Time Period	Title	Author	Level
Jesus—the center of God's salvation plan	*The Jesus Storybook Bible*	Sally Lloyd-Jones	E M
the name of Jesus—its origin, historic role, worldwide advance, and impact	*The Name*	Franklin Graham	M H
the big picture for understanding the New Testament	*Putting Together the Puzzle of the New Testament*	Bill Jones	M H
Roman-occupied Jerusalem; time of Christ	*A Sparrow Alone*	Alicia Peterson	E M
c. 30—death, burial, and resurrection of Christ	*The Passion of the Christ*	2004 film by Mel Gibson	H
Rome—Roman centurion; crucifixion	*The Robe* (based on novel by Lloyd C. Douglas)	1953 film starring Richard Burton	M H
Ancient Rome	*Demetrius and the Gladiator* (sequel to *The Robe*)	1954 film starring Anne Bancroft	M H
AD 30—Jerusalem at the time of Christ	*The Bronze Bow*	Elizabeth George Speare	E M
blind Roman beggar; Jesus of Nazareth	*Out of Darkness*	Alicia Petersen	E
35—church history; Paul; Benedict	*Peril and Peace: Vol. 1 Chronicles of the Ancient Church*	Mindy and Brandon Withrow	E
46–120—Greek historian, biographer of great men of virtue	*Plutarch's Lives*	Plutarch Arthur Hugh Clough, editor	M H
Arabic fairy tale	*Seven Daughters and Seven Sons*	Barbara Cohen	E
Roman persecution of the early saints	*The Martyr of the Catacombs: A Tale of Ancient Rome*	Anonymous	E
60—run away slave, Onesimus	*Twice Freed*	Patricia St. John	E
62—Ancient Britain and Rome; Roman invasion of Britain	*Beric the Briton: A Story of the Roman Invasion*	G. A. Henty	M H
62—Ancient Britain and Rome; Roman invasion of Britain	*Beric the Briton: A Story of the Roman Invasion* (audio storytelling recording)	Jim Weiss http://greathall.com	E M H
62—Ancient Britain and Rome; Roman invasion of Britain	*Beric the Briton: A Story of the Roman Invasion* (unabridged audio book)	Jim Hodges http://jimhodgesaudiobooks.com	E M H
Roman senator murdered	*The Ides of April*	Mary Ray	E
70—Palestine	*Beyond the Desert Gate* (sequel—*The Ides of April*)	Mary Ray	E
historical and theological roots; Christianity	*Apostolic Fathers*	J. B. Lightfoot and J. R. Harmer, editors	H

My design is not to write histories but lives ... so I must be allowed to give my more particular attention to the marks and indications of the souls of men .... Not only do they [lives] supply a mass of information, vividly and picturesquely presented, regarding the leading personalities of some of the greatest periods of the world's history, but they offer in concrete and inspiring form the ideals of human character in the antique world incarnated in a series of great heroic figures.

—Plutarch, *Plutarch's Lives*

Description or Time Period	Title	Author	Level
70–156—catacombs, amphitheatre, and persecution of Christians	*Polycarp: The Crown of Fire*	William Chad Newsom	E
70—fall of Jerusalem during the Palestinian revolt against Rome	*For the Temple: A Tale of the Fall of Jerusalem*	G. A. Henty	M H
70—fall of Jerusalem during the Palestinian revolt against Rome	*For the Temple: A Tale of the Fall of Jerusalem* (audio storytelling recording)	adapted and retold by Jim Weiss http://greathall.com	E M H
70—fall of Jerusalem during the Palestinian revolt against Rome	*For the Temple: A Tale of the Fall of Jerusalem* (unabridged audio book)	Jim Hodges http://jimhodgesaudiobooks.com	E M H
70—Jerusalem falls; firsthand account	*Story of the Last Days of Jerusalem*	Josephus; Alfred Church, editor	E
70—Jewish life	*Josephus: New Complete Works*	Flavius Josephus William Whiston, translator	H
79—Pompeii, Italy at the height of the Roman Empire	*The Last Days of Pompeii* (*Compact Classics: Vol. III*/p. 107)	Edward Bulwer-Lytton	H
OWN 79—Pompeii—volcanic explosion freezes ancient Italian city	*Pompeii: Buried Alive!*	Edith Kunhardt	E
100–165—Palestinian philosopher and Christian apologist; reason and truth	*First Apology*	Justin Martyr	H
119—legionnaire's son solves mystery; Ninth Roman Legion; barbarians; mountains of unconquered Scotland	*Eagle of the Ninth*	Rosemary Sutcliff	M H
119—legionnaire's son solves mystery; Ninth Roman Legion; barbarians; mountains of unconquered Scotland	*The Eagle* (based on the book by Rosemary Sutcliff)	2011 film starring Channing Tatum and Donald Sutherland	H
129—greatest doctor of the Roman Empire	*Galen and the Gateway to Medicine*	Jeanne Bendick	M
c. 140—profession of faith addressing Christ's humanity	*The Apostles' Creed*	apostles of the Early Church	M H
140–202—Smyrna—first great Catholic theologian attacks Gnosticism	*Against All Heresies*	Irenaeus	H
151–200—corruption of Roman government	*The Fall of the Roman Empire*	1964 film starring Alec Guinness, Sophia Loren and Christopher Plummer	H
160–225—North African theologian; the father of Latin theology	*Prescriptions Against Heretics*	Tertullian	H
161–180—last fruitful Roman Emperor	*Meditations* (*Compact Classics: Vol. II*/p. 375)	Marcus Aurelius	M H
Ancient Rome	*The History of the Decline and Fall of the Roman Empire*	Edward Gibbon	H
Ancient Rome	*Ancient Rome: How It Affects You Today*	Richard Maybury	E M
Ancient Greece; Rome; Britain	*The White Isle*	Caroline Dale Snedeker	M H

Marcus Aquila: He's not a slave. And he knows more about honor and freedom than you'll ever know.

—Rosemary Sutcliff, *The Eagle of the Ninth*

Description or Time Period	Title	Author	Level
history of Ireland	*How the Irish Saved Civilization: The Untold Story of Ireland's Heroic Role from the Fall of Rome to the Rise of Medieval Europe*	Thomas Cahill	H
185–254—early church father; answers criticisms against the Christian faith	*Contra Celsum*	Origen Henry Chadwick, translator	H
250–900—new Mayan settlements in America; ancient human sacrifice	*Kings of the Sun*	1963 film starring Yul Brynner	H
c. 260–340—linking the expansion of Rome to the success of the Christian faith	*Ecclesiastical History*	Eusebius	H
295–373—exiled Bishop of Alexandria defends the divinity of Christ	*On the Incarnation of the Word*	Athanasius	H
325—Nicaea; profession of faith; written to correct errors; deity of Christ	*The Nicene Creed*	First Council at Nicaea	H
339–397—Bishop of Milan; orthodoxy; church and state relations; led Augustine to convert to Christianity	*Letters, in Early Latin Theology*	Ambrose	H
347–420—Stridon; wrote on ascetism and the life of discipline	*Letters, in Early Latin Theology*	Jerome	H
354–430—God's people through history; progress of the Church	*The City of God*	Augustine of Hippo Henry Bettenson, translator	H
382–405—Bible translated from Hebrew and Aramaic into Latin	*The Bible: Latin Vulgate*	Jerome	H
401—autobiographical account; a life remade in the image of God; God's grace, beauty and providence	*The Confessions of St. Augustine* (*Compact Classics: Vol. II*/p. 355)	Augustine of Hippo Rex Warner, translator	H
406–453—Attila the Hun; Mongols bring down the mighty Roman Empire	*Sign of the Pagan*	1954 film starring Jack Palance and Alexander Scourby	H

A great civilization is not conquered from without until it has destroyed itself from within.

—*The Fall of the Roman Empire*

The Middle Ages

Timeline of Classics

Description or Time Period	Title	Author	Level
509 BC—from the fall of Rome to the Atomic Age; analysis of key moments, men, and ideas; influence on the condition and direction of our present culture	*How Should We Then Live: The Rise and Decline of Western Thought and Culture*	Francis A. Schaeffer http://labri.org/	H
ideas of the Renaissance and Reformation; cultural influence through the fine arts	*The Grandeur of Christianity—Part 2 (World Views of the Western World)*	David Quine http://cornerstonecurriculum.com	H
literature of Western culture	*The Norton Anthology of World Masterpieces*	Maynard Mack, general editor	H
Prehistoric to Post-Modern	*The Annotated Mona Lisa: A Crash Course in Art History From Prehistoric to Post-Modern*	Carol Strickland	M H
fifty volumes of selected world classics from all main divisions of literature	*Fifteen Minutes a Day Reading Guide for The Harvard Classics (1909)*	Charles W. Eliot, editor of *The Harvard Classics*	H
Shakespeare adapted for young readers	*Beautiful Stories from Shakespeare*	E. Nesbit	E M
Shakespeare adapted for young readers	*Tales from Shakespeare*	Charles and Mary Lamb	E M
Western civilization from prehistoric man through the modern nation-state; as told by a grandfather to his grandchildren	*The Story of Mankind*	Hendrick Willem van Loon (updated by Gerrit van Loon and John M. Merriman)	E M H
Western civilization from prehistoric man through the modern nation-state; as told by a grandfather to his grandchildren	*The Story of Mankind* (based on the book by Hendrick Willem van Loon)	1957 film adaptation starring the Marx Brothers and Ronald Colman	H
from the fall of Rome to the rise of the Renaissance	*The Story of the World Volume 2: The Middle Ages*	Susan Wise Bauer http://peacehillpress.com	E M
from the fall of Rome to the rise of the Renaissance	*The Story of the World Volume 2: The Middle Ages*	unabridged reading by Jim Weiss http://greathall.com	E M
10,000 BC to present	*The Kingfisher Atlas of World History: Pictorial Guide to the World's People and Events*	Simon Adams	E M H
flow of history from 5000 BC to modern times in a table format that includes history and politics, literature and theater, religion and philosophy, visual arts and music, science and technology, and daily life	*The Timetables of History: A Horizontal Linkage of People and Events* (directly translated from *Kulturfahrplan: The Culture Timetables*)	Bernard Grun	E M H
spiral-bound book of pages printed with a blank timeline; perfect for stickers, drawings, annotations, etc.	*Book of Time: Blank time line from 5000 BC to the present*	InquisiCorp Corporation http://sonlight.com	E M H

The Middle Ages included the millennium from the fifth to the fifteenth century, roughly from the fall of Rome until the Renaissance. During its initial period, called the Dark Ages, after the death of Byzantine Emperor Justinian ... until the reign of Charlemagne ... barbarians destroyed what had taken 3,000 years to build.

—Carol Strickland, *The Annotated Mona Lisa*

Description or Time Period	Title	Author	Level
Creation to Reformation; the New World	*Streams of Civilization* (Vol. 1)	Mary Stanton and Albert Hyma	E M
from earliest times to the present	*The Wall Chart of World History*	Barnes & Noble, Inc.	E M H
Middle Ages	*Famous Men of the Middle Ages*	Poland and Haaren	E
characters and events of the Middle Ages who shaped Western civilization	*Twelve Bright Trumpets*	Margaret Leighton	E
Ancients and Medieval to the Modern Era	*The Picture History of Great Inventors*	Gillian Clements	E M H
collection of short stories; famous authors	*Faerie Gold: Treasures from the Lands of Enchantment*	Kathryn Lindskoog and Ranelda Mack Hunsicker, editors	E
reference guide to understanding our culture through great Western literary classics	*Invitation to the Classics: A Guide to Books You've Always Wanted to Read*	Louise Cowan and Os Guinness, editors	M H
Medieval	*Castle*	David Macaulay	M
Medieval	*Castle: Discover the Mysteries of the Medieval Castle*	DK Eyewitness Book http://us.dk.com	E M
Medieval battles, banquets, sieges, and chivalry	*Knight: Discover the World of the Medieval Knight*	DK Eyewitness Book http://us.dk.com	E M
Medieval England; knighthood	*Men of Iron*	Howard Pyle	E M
Medieval knighthood	*The Making of a Knight*	Patrick O'Brien	E
Middle Ages	*Otto of the Silver Hand*	Howard Pyle, writer and illustrator	E M
480–547—Italy; rule of life for monks	*Rule of St. Benedict in English*	Benedict of Nursia; T. Fry, trans.	H
5th century—barbarian invasion of Britain; Roman legionnaire fights to save his land	*The Lantern Bearers*	Rosemary Sutcliff	E
5th century—Iceland; barbarians	*Story of Rolf and the Viking Bow*	Allen French	E
5th century Greece; Athens; Sparta	*Theras and His Town*	Caroline Dale Snedeker	E
5th century—Britain; Celts; Saxons; King Arthur; beginnings of the British cavalry	*Black Horses for the King*	Anne McCaffrey	E
c. 480–524—Medieval Europe	*The Consolation of Philosophy*	Boethius	H
early 6th century—Venice, Cyprus; romantic tragedy	*Othello (Compact Classics: Vol. I5-H5)*	William Shakespeare	H
early 6th century—Venice, Cyprus; romantic tragedy	*Othello* (based on the play by William Shakespeare)	1965 British film version starring Laurence Olivier	H

For two hundred years knights have fought and died for a land not our own. But on that day at Badon Hill, all who fought put our lives in service of a greater cause: Freedom. And as for the knights who gave their lives, their deaths were cause for neither mourning nor sadness. For they live forever, their names and deeds handed down from father to son, mother to daughter, in the Legends of King Arthur and his knights.

—Sir Thomas Malory, *Tales of King Arthur*

Description or Time Period	Title	Author	Level
6th century Britain; legendary Knights of the Round Table	*Tales of King Arthur* (*Compact Classics: Vol. III*/p. 41)	Sir Thomas Malory	H
lore of King Arthur begins here	*History of the Kings of Britain*	Geoffrey of Monmouth	M H
6th century England—during the reign of King Arthur; social satire	*A Connecticut Yankee in King Arthur's Court* (*Compact Classics: Vol. I*/5-G3)	Mark Twain	H
King Arthur; Knights of the Round Table	*The Sword and the Circle*	Rosemary Sutcliff	M
King Arthur; Knights of the Round Table	*The Story of King Arthur and His Knights*	Howard Pyle	M H
King Arthur's knights; Round Table	*The Sword in the Tree*	Clyde Robert Bulla	E M
King Arthur; Camelot; Guinevere; Merlyn	*The Once and Future King*	Terence Hanbury White	H
King Arthur; Guinevere; Lancelot; Merlin; honor, loyalty, courage, and chivalry	*King Arthur*	Roger Lancelyn Green	E
c. 600—Britain (near modern-day Edinburgh and Yorkshire) 300 warriors trained to defend against Saxon invaders	*The Shining Company* (based on the earliest surviving poem of North Britain; raid recorded by actual survivor)	Rosemary Sutcliff	M
c. 673–735—history records God's supervision over human affairs	*Ecclesiastical History of the English People*	Bede	H
c. 700–750—Anglo-Saxon; first great English epic poem; influences of rapidly growing Christianity on a warrior society	*Beowulf* (*Compact Classics: Vol. I*/5-B2)	poet unknown Seamus Heaney, translator	M H
c. 700–750—pagan religions; Christianity	*Beowulf: An Updated Verse Translation*	Frederick Rebsamen	E M H
8th century—Germany; medieval Esther	*The Princess Adelina*	Julie Sutter	E
742–814—France; writings on the personal life and campaigns of Charlemagne	*Two Lives of Charlemagne*	Einhard and Notker the Stammerer	H
742–814—France	*Stories of Charlemagne*	Jennifer Westwood	M H
778—France; the attack of the rearguard of Charlemagne's army	*The Song of Roland*	anonymous poet Dorothy Sayers, translator	M H
Middle Ages	*Mythology: Age of Fable, Chivalry, and Charlemagne*	Thomas Bulfinch	H
late 700s—founding of the Holy Roman Empire	*Son of Charlemagne*	Barbara Willard	E
late 700–1100s—Boy learns to read in order to tell of his adventures.	*Viking Adventure*	Clyde Robert Bulla	E
800s—Norsemen raids; Europe	*Viking Times*	Anthony Mason	E M

Ah, gentlemen of noble strain, I trust thee unto God the true, whose service never man shall do with more devoted heart and mind: to guard the faith, to win mankind.
—Anonymous Poet, *The Song of Roland*

Description or Time Period	Title	Author	Level
800s—Scandinavia	*Adventures With the Vikings*	Linda Bailey	E
Vikings battling Moors	*The Long Ships*	1964 film starring Sidney Poitier	H
Vikings; barbaric society—filmed on site in Normandy and Brittany	*The Vikings* (narrated by Orson Welles)	1958 film starring Kirk Douglas and Tony Curtis	H
Vikings	*Leif the Lucky*	Ingri and Edgar Parin D'Aulaire	E
871–899—Beloved king defended Anglo-Saxon England from Viking raids.	*The Dragon and The Raven: The Days of King Alfred and the Viking Invasion*	G. A. Henty	M H
871–899—Beloved king defended Anglo-Saxon England from Viking raids.	*The Dragon and The Raven: The Days of King Alfred and the Viking Invasion* (unabridged audio book)	Jim Hodges http://jimhodgesaudiobooks.com	E M H
9th century—defender against Viking invaders; revival of learning and Christianity	*Alfred the Great* (king of Wessex)	Asser; Simon Keynes and Michael Lapidge, translators	H
Medieval Christianity	*Anselm of Canterbury: The Major Works*	St. Anselm; Davies and Evans, ed.	H
800–900—Persia; Shahrazad	*Shadow Spinner*	Susan Fletcher	E
800–900—Persia; Shahrazad	*Aladdin and Other Favorite Arabian Nights Stories*	Phillip Smith	E
Medieval Arabia—Persia	*Arabian Nights* (audio storytelling recording)	Jim Weiss http://greathall.com	E M H
Medieval, imaginative	*Redwall*	Brian Jacques	M H
Medieval England; tragic drama	*King Lear* (*Compact Classics: Vol. I*/5-H2)	William Shakespeare	H
Medieval England; time of King Arthur	*The Two Collars*	Jeri Massi	E
Medieval	*The Bridge* (book 1 of the Bracken trilogy)	Jeri Massi	E
Medieval	*Crown and Jewel* (book 2 of the Bracken trilogy)	Jeri Massi	E
Medieval battle	*Theobald the Iron-Hearted*	E. Thompson Baird	M
late Medieval period; known as one of the greatest narrative English poems	*The Rime of the Ancient Mariner* (*Compact Classics: Vol. I*/5-D1)	Samuel Taylor Coleridge Gustave Dore—illustrator	H
Medieval and Renaissance literature	*Fierce Wars and Faithful Loves*	Edmund Spenser; Roy Maynard, ed.	H
Renaissance—Italian master painter	*The Apprentice*	Pilar Molina Llorente	E
Renaissance; Leonardo da Vinci	*The Second Mrs. Giaconda*	E. L. Konigsburg	E
Renaissance	*Leonardo da Vinci*	Emily Hahn	E

For in prosperity a man is often puffed up with pride, whereas tribulations chasten and humble him through suffering and sorrow. In the midst of prosperity the mind is elated, and in prosperity a man forgets himself; in hardship he is forced to reflect on himself, even though he be unwilling. In prosperity a man often destroys the good he has done; amidst difficulties he often repairs what he long since did in the way of wickedness.

—King Alfred the Great

Description or Time Period	Title	Author	Level
Renaissance—Venice, Italy	*The Merchant of Venice* (*Compact Classics: Vol. I*/5-I4)	William Shakespeare	H
970–1020—Leif Erikson; Norway; Iceland; prisoners of Viking raiders	*Viking Quest Series*	Lois Walfrid Johnson	E
1066—Norman conquest; Battle of Hastings	*The King's Shadow*	Elizabeth Alder	E
1066—Britain and Normandy	*Wulf the Saxon: A Story of the Norman Conquest*	G. A. Henty	M H
1066—Britain and Normandy	*Wulf the Saxon: A Story of the Norman Conquest* (audio storytelling recording)	adapted and retold by Jim Weiss http://greathall.com	E M H
1066—Britain and Normandy	*Wulf the Saxon: A Story of the Norman Conquest* (unabridged audio recording)	Jim Hodges http://jimhodgesaudiobooks.com	E M H
11th century Scotland—tragedy of ambition, betrayal, superstition and murder	*Macbeth (Compact Classics: Vol. I/5 H4)*	William Shakespeare Roma Gill, editor	M H
11th century Scotland—tragedy	*Macbeth*	1948 film starring Orson Welles	H
1090–1153—abbot; Second Crusade	*Selected Works*	Bernard of Clairvaux	H
1095–1272—the Crusades; uniting England	*The Merry Adventures of Robin Hood*	Howard Pyle	M H
1095–1272—the Crusades	*Tales of Robin Hood*	Tony Allan	E
1095–1272—the Crusades	*The Adventures of Robin Hood*	film starring Olivia de Havilland and Errol Flynn	H
1100s—England	*Robin Hood* (audio storytelling recording)	Jim Weiss http://greathall.com	E M H
1122—France; England; Eleanor of Aquitaine	*Queen Eleanor: Independent Spirit of the Medieval World*	Polly Brooks	M
1154–1189—France; England—wife of two kings, mother of two others	*A Proud Taste for Scarlet and Miniver* (story of Eleanor of Aquitaine, wife of King Henry II)	E. L. Konigsburg	E M
1157–1199—England; Third Crusade	*Winning His Spurs: A Story of the Crusades*	George Alfred Henty	H
1162–1227—NE Asia	*Genghis Khan and the Mongol Horde*	Harold Lamb	E
1170—Canterbury, England; King Henry II; murder of the Archbishop of Canterbury	*Murder in the Cathedral* (*Compact Classics: Vol. II/p. 67)*	T. S. Eliot	H

But Robin Hood stayed hidden in Sherwood Forest for one year, gathering around him many other outlaws like himself. Some were wanted for hunting the King's deer in cold winter when they had no food; some had been taxed so heavily they had no money to live; and some had been turned out of their farms so that their land might be added to the King's property in Sherwood Forest. All had come to escape the unfair treatment they had been given at the hands of the King.

—Howard Pyle, *The Merry Adventures of Robin Hood*

Description or Time Period	Title	Author	Level
1170—Canterbury, England; King Henry II; murder of the Archbishop of Canterbury	*Becket* (story of Thomas Becket)	1964 film starring Peter O'Toole and Richard Burton	H
1182–1226	*Saint Francis*	Brian Wildsmith	E
1188–1192—King Richard	*Winning His Spurs: A Tale of the Crusades*	G. A. Henty	M H
1188–1192—King Richard	*Winning His Spurs: A Tale of the Crusades* (unabridged audio recording)	Jim Hodges http://jimhodgesaudiobooks.com	E M H
1190–1200—epic German poem; legendary conflict between Burgundians and Huns (Attila)	*Nibelungenlied* (first and most popular German contribution to European literature)	Anonymous poet—oral tradition	H
1195—France; Middle Ages	*The Minstrel in the Tower*	Gloria Skurzynski	E M
12th century Korea	*A Single Shard*	Linda Sue Park	M H
late 12th century England; crusades; Richard the Lion Heart; Prince John; Lady Rowena	*Ivanhoe* (*Compact Classics: Vol. III*/p. 45)	Sir Walter Scott	H
12th century—crossing Europe and Asia	*The Walking Drum*	Louis L'Amour	H
1200—Fourth Crusade	*Chronicles of the Crusades*	Joinville and Villehardouin Margaret Shaw, translator	H
1200—Cornwall—setting for the Magna Charta; King Richard is dead; John is king.	*The Lost Baron*	Allen French	E
c. 1200—Elsinore, Denmark; tragic drama; murder based on a legend found in the History of the Danes written about 1200 by Saxo Grammaticus	*Hamlet, Prince of Denmark* (*Compact Classics: Vol. I/5–H1*)	William Shakespeare	H
1215—English history; wicked King John	*The Magna Charta*	James Daugherty	M H
1215—Magna Carta; founding and colonization of America	*The Story of Liberty*	Charles Coffin (reprinted from the original 1879 transcript)	H
1217–1274—Italian friar, administrator, professor, and cardinal	*The Soul's Journey into God*	Bonaventure	H
13th century England	*Adam of the Road*	Elizabeth Janet Gray	M
European Immigration to N. America	*They Sought a New World*	William Kurelek	E M
1254–1324—Venice; Asia; 24-year journey	*Marco Polo: The Boy Who Traveled the Medieval World*	Nick McCarty	E
1254–1324—Venice; Italy; E. China; autobiographical	*The Travels of Marco Polo* (*Compact Classics: Vol. I/5-C4*)	Marco Polo	M H
1254—Venice, Italy; confidant of Kublai Khan	*Marco Polo*	Charles P. Graves	E M

It is dangerous for men in power if no one dares to tell them when they go wrong.
—Thomas Becket

Description or Time Period	Title	Author	Level
c. 1265–1274—medieval friar/professor uses Aristotelian logic to explain Christian doctrines: incarnation, sacraments, etc.	*Summa Theologica*	Thomas Aquinas	H
1296–1305—Scots vs. King Edward; William Wallace and Robert the Bruce	*The Scottish Chiefs*	Jane Porter	H
1285—heraldry, weaponry, feudal system	*Castle Diary: The Journal of Tobias Burgess*	Richard Platt	E
1291—Swiss revolt against Austrian oppression	*William Tell*	Leonard Everett Fisher	E
1296–1314—Scotland's battle for independence from England	*In Freedom's Cause: A Story of Wallace and Bruce*	George Alfred Henty	M H
1296–1314—Scotland's battle for independence from England	*In Freedom's Cause: A Story of Wallace and Bruce* (audio storytelling recording)	adapted and retold by Jim Weiss http://greathall.com	E M H
1296–1314—Scotland's battle for independence from England	*In Freedom's Cause: A Story of Wallace and Bruce* (unabridged audio recording)	Jim Hodges http://jimhodgesaudiobooks.com	E M H
c. 1307–1321—Florence, Italy; Medieval Christendom; sacred poem portraying the human soul discovering the life of faith in a faithless world	*The Divine Comedy Inferno, Purgatorio, and Paradiso* (Compact Classics: Vol. I/5-B4)	Dante Alighieri Dorothy L. Sayers, translator (3-volume Penguin edition)	M H
1307—Germany; legend of William Tell	*The Apple and the Arrow*	Mary and Conrad Buff	E
1300s—England; knighthood	*The Door in the Wall*	Marguerite de Angeli	M
1320s–1384—Oxford, England	*Morning Star of the Reformation: John Wycliffe and the English Translation of the Bible*	Andy Thomson	E
1342–1416—Norwich, England; devotional writings	*Revelations of Divine Love*	Julian of Norwich	H
c. 1370—British Medieval; one of earliest and finest accounts of King Arthur's court	*Sir Gawain and the Green Knight*	Anonymous author; J.R.R. Tolkien, translator	M H
1377—England; historical narrative	*Crispin: The Cross of Lead*	Avi	M
1380—Venice, Italy—the balance of European power and trade	*The Lion of St. Mark* (audio storytelling recording)	Jim Weiss http://greathall.com	E M H
1380s—England; translated into common English	*The Holy Bible*	John Wycliffe	E M H
c. 1386–1400—Britain; pilgrims traveling to Canterbury	*The Canterbury Tales* (Compact Classics: Vol. III/p. 105)	Geoffrey Chaucer Nevill Coghill, translator	M H
14th century English literature	*Chanticleer and the Fox*	Geoffrey Chaucer; Barbara Cooney	E M

Twice in our century has this, our heritage, been in deadly peril and has been preserved at untold cost. When we know the story of how our liberties were won and at what price, we will value and guard them, for they are not ours alone. They bear no national label—they belong to all Mankind.

—Barons of King John, *The Magna Charta*

Description or Time Period	Title	Author	Level
14th century	*Canterbury Quintet* (reader-friendly edition)	Geoffrey Chaucer	H
14th century—Reformation	*How the Reformation Happened*	Hilaire Belloc	M H
1400s—Paris, France	*Marguerite Makes a Book*	Bruce Robertson	E
1400s—insanity of 15th century British king	*Richard III* (based on the play by William Shakespeare)	1955 British film starring Laurence Olivier	H
1412–1431—France; peasant; national heroine	*Joan of Arc: Warrior Saint*	Jay Williams	E
1412–1431—France	*Joan of Arc*	Mark Twain	H
1412–1431—France	*Joan of Arc*	Hilaire Belloc	H
1418–1427—devotional meditations on the life and teachings of Jesus Christ; rated second only to the Bible for guidance and inspiration	*The Imitation of Christ* (Compact Classics: Vol. II/p. 357)	Thomas a Kempis	H
1438—architectural, engineering, mathematical, and astronomical advances; three major civilizations prior to European presence in the New World	*Incans, Aztecs & Mayans*	John Holzmann	E M
1440—Gutenberg printing press revolutionized the printing of books; religion and science texts spread rapidly.	*Ink on His Fingers*	Louise A. Vernon	E

Thus, in an altogether unique way, Dante summarizes the literature, the philosophy, the science, and the religion of the Middle Ages. Through the intensity of his capacity for experience, the splendor of his power of expression, and the depth of his spiritual and philosophic insight, he at once sums up and transcends a whole era of human history.

—Charles W. Eliot, editor, *The Harvard Classics: The Divine Comedy of Dante*

Epidemics swept away the people like flies, and the burials were conducted secretly by night; for public funerals were not allowed, lest the revelation of the magnitude of the plague's work unman the people and plunge them into despair.

—Mark Twain, *Joan of Arc*

Renaissance and Reformation

Timeline of Classics

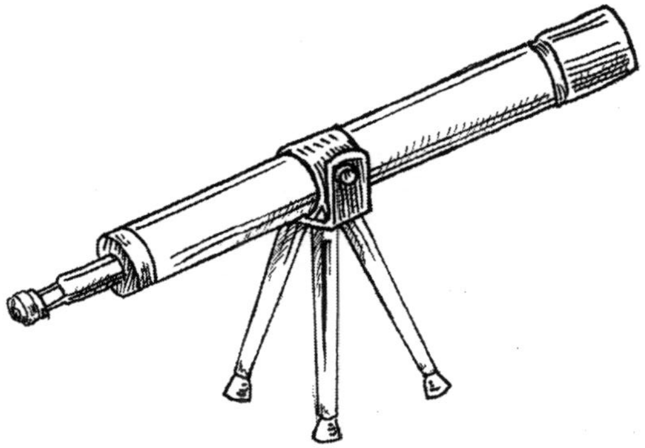

Description or Time Period	Title	Author	Level
flow of history from 5000 BC to modern times in a table format that includes history and politics, literature and theater, religion and philosophy, visual arts and music, science and technology, and daily life	*The Timetables of History: A Horizontal Linkage of People and Events* (directly translated from *Kulturfahrplan: The Culture Timetables)*	Bernard Grun; based on the work of Werner Stein and Wallace Brockway	E M H
from Elizabeth I to the Forty-Niners	*The Story of the World Volume 3: Early Modern Times*	Susan Wise Bauer http://peacehillpress.com	E M
from Elizabeth I to the Forty-Niners	*The Story of the World Volume 3: Early Modern Times*	unabridged reading by Jim Weiss http://greathall.com	E M
spiral-bound book of pages printed with a blank timeline; perfect for stickers, drawings, annotations, etc.	*Book of Time: Blank time line from 5000 BC to the present*	InquisiCorp Corporation http://sonlight.com	E M H
from earliest times to the present	*The Wall Chart of World History*	Barnes & Noble, Inc.	E M H
Western civilization from prehistoric man through the modern nation-state; as told by a grandfather to his grandchildren	*The Story of Mankind*	Hendrick Willem van Loon (updated by Gerrit van Loon and John M. Merriman)	E M
Western civilization from prehistoric man through the modern nation-state; as told by a grandfather to his grandchildren	*The Story of Mankind* (based on the book by Hendrick Willem van Loon)	1957 film adaptation featuring the Marx Brothers and Ronald Colman	H
founding fathers, presidents, and statesmen	*America's God and Country: Encyclopedia of Quotations*	William J. Federer	E M H
founding of America	*America's Providential History*	Mark Beliles and Stephen McDowell	H
reference guide to understanding culture through great Western literary classics	*Invitation to the Classics: A Guide to Books You've Always Wanted to Read*	Louise Cowan and Os Guinness, editors	M H
literature of Western Culture through the Renaissance	*The Norton Anthology of World Masterpieces Vol. 1*	Maynard Mack, general editor	H
Shakespeare adapted for children	*Beautiful Stories from Shakespeare*	Edith Nesbit	E M
Shakespeare adapted for children	*Tales from Shakespeare*	Charles and Mary Lamb	E M
prehistory to Post-Modern era	*The Annotated Mona Lisa: A Crash Course in Art History From Prehistoric to Post-Modern*	Carol Strickland	M H
fifty volumes of selected world classics from all main divisions of literature	*Fifteen Minutes a Day Reading Guide for The Harvard Classics* (1909)	Charles W. Eliot editor of *The Harvard Classics*	H
1451–1506—Italy	*Columbus*	Ingri and Edgar D'Aulaire	E M

In the beginning of the contest with Britain, when we were sensible of danger, we had daily prayers in this room for Divine protection. Our prayers, Sir, were heard and they were graciously answered. All of us who were engaged in the struggle must have observed frequent instances of a superintending Providence in our favor … . Have we now forgotten this powerful Friend? Or do we imagine we no longer need His assistance?

—Benjamin Franklin, addressing the Constitutional Convention, 1787

Description or Time Period	Title	Author	Level
1451–1506—biography of Italian explorer	*A History of the Life and Voyages of Christopher Columbus*	Washington Irving	H
1451–1506—Italian explorer	*The World of Columbus and Sons*	Genevieve Foster	M H
1451–1506—Italian explorer	*Christopher Columbus: "Master Sailor and Explorer" (Compact Classics: Vol. I/4-E4)*	Biography: Leaders of the Spirit	E H
1451–1506—biography of Italian explorer	*Admiral of the Ocean Sea: A Life of Christopher Columbus*	Samuel Eliot Morison	M H
1452–1519—Italy; pioneer inventor and artist	*Leonardo da Vinci*	Diane Stanley	E
1452–1519—pursuits and inventions	*Leonardo: Beautiful Dreamer*	Robert Byrd	E
1452–1519—Italy	*Leonardo da Vinci "Renaissance Man" (Compact Classics: Vol. I/4-C2)*	Biography: Artists and Philosophers	M H
1466–1536—Desiderius Erasmus of Rotterdam	*The Man Who Laid the Egg*	Louise A. Vernon	E
1466–1536—abuses of Medieval church; Renaissance Christian humanist	*The Praise of Folly*	Erasmus	H
1470–1480—Italian coast is defended against Muslim attackers	*A Knight of the White Cross: A Tale of the Siege of Rhodes*	G. A. Henty	M H
1470–1480—Italian coast is defended against Muslim attackers	*A Knight of the White Cross: A Tale of the Siege of Rhodes* (unabridged audio book)	Jim Hodges http://jimhodgesaudiobooks.com	E M H
1473–1543—Torun, Poland	*Nicolaus Copernicus "Religious Astronomer" (Compact Classics: Vol. I/4-A4)*	Biography: Pioneers in Science	H
Renaissance Europe	*Galileo and the Stargazers: Copernicus, Brahe, Kepler, and Galileo* (audio storytelling recording)	Jim Weiss http://greathall.com	E M H
1473—Korea	*The Kite Fighters*	Linda Sue Park	E
1475–1564—Italy	*Michelangelo "Artist" (Compact Classics: Vol. I/4-C4)*	Biography: Artists and Philosophers	H
1475–1564—Italian sculptor, painter, architect	*Michelangelo—Man of the Renaissance*	Diane Stanley	E M
1478–1535—Renaissance Christian humanist	*The Life of Sir Thomas More*	William Roper	H

I have always read that the world, both land and water, was spherical, as the authority and researches of Ptolemy and all the others who have written on this subject demonstrate and prove, as do the eclipses of the moon and other experiments that are made from east to west, and the elevation of the North Star from north to south.

—Christopher Columbus, Third Voyage, October 18, 1498

Description or Time Period	Title	Author	Level
1480–1521—Portuguese explorer; circled the globe	*Ferdinand Magellan*	S. A. Kramer	E
1483–1546—Germany; Luther; Reformation	*Luther the Leader*	Virgil Robinson	E
1483–1546—Germany	*Here I Stand: A Life of Martin Luther*	Roland H. Bainton	H
1483–1546—Germany—changed the history of the Western world	*Luther: Biography of a Reformer*	Frederick Nohl	M H
Europe—Reformation	*The Grandeur of Christianity (World Views of the Western World)*	David Quine	H
1483–1546—Germany; salvation	*The Bondage of the Will*	Martin Luther; J. I. Packer and O. R. Johnston, translators	M H
15th century France; gypsy girl saved by the deformed ringer of cathedral bells	*The Hunchback of Notre Dame (Compact Classics: Vol. II/p. 143)*	Victor Hugo	H
15th century France	*The Hunchback of Notre Dame*	1939 film starring Charles Laughton	H
15th century—Spain; Protestant Reformation	*My Escape from the Auto De Fe*	W. M. Timms	E
15th century—England; Protestant Reformation	*The Hawk that Dare Not Hunt by Day* (story of William Tyndale)	Scott O'Dell	M H
15th century—Poland; loyalty and bravery against invading Tartars	*Trumpeter of Krakow*	Eric P. Kelly	M H
15th century—remote island	*The Tempest (Compact Classics: Vol. I/5-I2)*	William Shakespeare	H
15th and 16th centuries	*Explorers Who Got Lost*	Diane Sansevere Dreher	E
1400s—Renaissance Italy—Dispute between families ends in tragedy for young lovers.	*Romeo and Juliet (Compact Classics: Vol. I/5-H3)*	William Shakespeare	H
1400s—Renaissance Italy—Dispute between families ends in tragedy for young lovers.	*Romeo and Juliet* (audio storytelling recording)	adapted and retold by Jim Weiss http://greathall.com	E M H
1400s—Renaissance Italy—Dispute between families ends in tragedy for young lovers.	*Romeo and Juliet* (based on the play by William Shakespeare)	1968 British-Italian film starring Michael York	M H
1491–1547—England; Ireland; Mary Tudor describes her father, Henry VIII.	*Mary, Bloody Mary*	Carolyn Meyer	E M
1492—Columbus' journey	*Pedro's Journal*	Pam Conrad	M H
1492—ship's log; Columbus	*First Voyage to America*	Christopher Columbus	E M
1492–1503—letters and selected documents; Italian explorer traveled from Spain to the Western hemisphere.	*Four Voyages to the New World*	Christopher Columbus	H

I do not feel obliged to believe that the same God who has endowed us with sense, reason, and intellect has intended us to forgo their use.

—Galileo Galilei

Description or Time Period	Title	Author	Level
1492–2001—America	*A Patriot's History of the United States: From Columbus's Great Discovery to the War on Terror*	Larry Schweikart and Michael Allen	H
1492–1789—God's plan for America	*The Light and the Glory*	Peter Marshall and David Manuel	E M
providential history of the United States	*Under God*	Toby Mac	H
16th century—Tudor King of England	*Henry VIII (Compact Classics: Vol. I/5-C3)*	William Shakespeare	M H
16th century—England; Italy; farcical comedy	*The Taming of the Shrew (Compact Classics: Vol. I; 511)*	William Shakespeare	M H
16th century—Renaissance Italy	*Shakespeare for Children: The Taming of the Shrew* (audio storytelling recording)	adapted and retold by Jim Weiss http://greathall.com	E M H
16th century—opposing Scottish clans; Celtic Highlanders vs. Saxon Lowlanders loyal to the King	*The Lady of the Lake (Compact Classics: Vol. I/5-C2)*	Sir Walter Scott	M H
16th century—Italy	*Much Ado About Nothing (Compact Classics: Vol. I/5-I5)*	William Shakespeare	H
16th century—Italy	*Much Ado About Nothing* (based on the play by William Shakespeare)	1992 British-U.S. film starring Michael Keaton	H
16th century—Japan	*The Samurai's Tale*	Erik Christian Haugaard	E
Renaissance and Reformation	*The World of Columbus and Sons*	Genevieve Foster	M H
1509–1564—France	*John Calvin*	Simonetta Carr	E
1509–1564—France	*The Life of John Calvin*	Theodore Beza; Gary Sanseri, editor	E
1509–1564—France	*Institutes of the Christian Religion*	John Calvin; John T. McNeill, editor	H
1510–1572—tyranny and corruption; father of Scottish Presbyterianism	*For Kirk and Covenant: The Stalwart Courage of John Knox*	Douglas Wilson	E
1515–1547—France; Protestant Reformation; John Calvin	*The River of Grace*	Joyce McPherson	E
1515—Italy	*A Treasury of Wisdom: Raphael and Michelangelo* (audio storytelling recording)	Jim Weiss http://greathall.com	E M H
1516—Renaissance modern epoch reviving utopian ideas for perfecting the human condition	*Utopia (Compact Classics: Vol. I/5-M4)*	Sir Thomas More	H
1517—Castle Church; Wittenberg, Germany; protest against clerical abuses; sparked Reformation	*The Ninety-Five Theses (Compact Classics: Vol. II/p. 359)*	Martin Luther	H

At once each family began to cast blame upon the other for the tragedy. The Friar, however, stepped forward and explained the circumstances which had led to the deaths of their tender children, whose only sin was to have loved.

—William Shakespeare, *Romeo and Juliet*

Description or Time Period	Title	Author	Level
1519–1559—archbishop vs. King Henry II	*If All the Swords in England: A Story of Thomas Becket*	Barbara Willard	E
1520—spark of the Reformation	*The Babylonian Captivity of the Church*	Martin Luther	H
1521—Spaniards overcome Aztec Empire.	*By Right of Conquest: With Cortez in Mexico*	G. A. Henty	M H
1521—Small group of Spaniards overcomes Aztec Empire.	*By Right of Conquest: With Cortez in Mexico* (unabridged audio book)	Jim Hodges http://jimhodgesaudiobooks.com	E M H
1529—spark of the Reformation	*The Small Catechism*	Martin Luther	H
1500s—British-Spanish conflict; Armada	*Fire Over England*	1937 film starring Vivien Leigh	H
1532—modern political philosophy; turn from virtue to power, success, image and efficiency	*The Prince (Compact Classics: Vol. I/5-K3)*	Niccolo Machiavelli George Bull, translator	H
Spanish inquisition—Phillip II	*The Adventures of Don Juan*	1948 Oscar winner starring Errol Flynn and Raymond Burr	H
1533–1603—Queen Elizabeth I of England	*Good Queen Bess: The Story of Elizabeth I of England*	Diane Stanley and Peter Vennema	E
1533–1584—Nassau; Protestant hero	*William of Orange*	W. G. Van de Hulst	E
1534—forming the Church of England; Henry VIII; conflict of conscience	*A Man for All Seasons*	1966 British film	H
1536—French scholar pens an honest view of God and the human condition.	*Institutes of the Christian Religion (Compact Classics: Vol. II/p. 361)*	John Calvin	H
1545—Iga Mountains, Japan	*Blue Fingers: A Ninja's Tale*	Cheryl Aylward Whitesel	M
1547—England—Prince of Wales switches places with a common pauper.	*The Prince and the Pauper (Compact Classics: Vol. I/5-G5)*	Mark Twain	H
1547—England—Prince of Wales switches places with a common pauper.	*The Prince and the Pauper* (audio storytelling recording)	adapted and retold by Jim Weiss http://greathall.com	E M H
1547—England—Prince of Wales switches places with a common pauper.	*The Prince and the Pauper* (based on the book by Mark Twain)	1937 film starring Errol Flynn	E M H
1552–1618—France; England; Roanoke Island; young spy for Sir Walter Raleigh	*Raleigh's Page*	Alan Armstrong	E M

And though this world, with devils filled, should threaten to undo us; we will not fear, for God hath willed His truth to triumph through us. The prince of darkness grim, we tremble not for him; his rage we can endure, for lo! His doom is sure; one little word shall fell him.

—Martin Luther, "A Mighty Fortress Is Our God"

Description or Time Period	Title	Author	Level
1561—Netherlands; confession of faith; 37 articles detailing the doctrines of God, etc.	*The Belgic Confession*	Guido de Bres	H
1563—Germany; Protestant reformed confession in the form of 129 Q and A regarding the misery, deliverance, and gratitude of man	*The Heidelberg Catechism*	Caspar Olevianus and Zacharias Ursinus	M H
1564–1642—Florence, Italy; life of Galileo; scientist, physicist, and mathematician	*Starry Messenger*	Peter Sis	E
1564–1642—Renaissance	*Along Came Galileo*	Jeanne Bendick	E
1564–1642	*The Great Physicists from Galileo to Einstein*	George Gamow	H
1564–1642—Renaissance; Florence, Italy	*Galileo Galilei: Astronomer and Scientist (Compact Classics: Vol. I/4-A3)*	Biography: Pioneers in Science	M H
1564–1616—England SCM	*Bard of Avon: The Story of William Shakespeare*	Diane Stanley	E M
1564–1616—England; introduction to Shakespeare	*Tales from Shakespeare*	Charles and Mary Lamb	E M
1564–1616—England SCM	*Shakespeare for Children*	Charles and Mary Lamb	E M
1564–1616—England	*DK Eyewitness Books: Shakespeare*	Peter Chrisp	E M
1564–1616—England	*William Shakespeare "Master Poet and Dramatist" (Compact Classics: Vol. I/4-C1)*	Biography: Artists and Philosophers	M H
1564–1616—England SCM	*William Shakespeare and the Globe*	Aliki	E M
1564–1616—England	*The Sonnets of Shakespeare*	William Shakespeare	M H
1564–1616—England	*The Shakespeare Stealer*	Gary Blackwood	E
1564–1616—England	*Shakespeare's Scribe* (sequel to *The Shakespeare Stealer*)	Gary Blackwood	E
1567–1622—Geneva; devotional writings; presence of God; sacredness of life	*Introduction to the Devout Life*	Francis of Sales	H
1572–1631—England	*The Sonnets of John Donne (Compact Classics: Vol. II/p. 237)*	John Donne	H
1580—Spanish Armada and Inquisition	*The Queen's Pirate: The Adventures of Queen Elizabeth I and Sir Francis Drake, Explorer Extraordinaire* (audio storytelling recording)	Jim Weiss http://greathall.com	E M H

When I am king, they shall not have bread and shelter only, but also teachings out of books; for a full belly is little worth where the mind is starved.

—Mark Twain, *The Prince and the Pauper*

Description or Time Period	Title	Author	Level
1584—Ireland; Elizabethan English conflict	*Red Hugh, Prince of Donegal*	Robert T. Reilly	M
1590–1657—England	*William Bradford: Pilgrim Boy*	Bradford Smith	E
1500s France—romantic comedy	*As You Like It (Compact Classics: Vol. I/5-13)*	William Shakespeare	H
1594–1596—written	*A Midsummer Night's Dream*	William Shakespeare	M H
1594–1596—best film version for children; features music by Mendelssohn	*A Midsummer Night's Dream*	1935 film version starring Olivia de Havilland	E M H
1590s—England	*The Sonnets of William Shakespeare (Compact Classics: Vol. II/p. 235)*	William Shakespeare	M H
1595–1617—Pocahontas; John Smith	*The Captive Princess*	Wendy Lawton	E
1595—Pocahontas; first American heroine	*American Heroes*	Marfé Ferguson Delano	E M H
16th–17th centuries—Puritans	*Worldly Saints*	Leland Ryken	E M
16th–17th centuries—Puritans	*Visible Saints: The History of a Puritan Idea*	Edmund S. Morgan	E M
1600–1740—America	*A History of US (2) Making Thirteen Colonies*	Joy Hakim	E M
1600–1990—Baroque Period–Modern Era	*The Story of the Orchestra*	Robert Levine	E M
Renaissance	*Milton Cross' New Encyclopedia of the Great Composers and Their Music*	Milton Cross and David Ewen	M H
Renaissance Italy	*Masters of the Renaissance* (audio storytelling recording)	Jim Weiss http://greathall.com	E M H
Renaissance Venice	*The Merchant of Venice (Compact Classics: Vol. I/p.514)*	William Shakespeare	M H
Ancients and Medieval to the Modern Era	*The Picture History of Great Inventors*	Gillian Clements	E M H
17th century—Seville, Spain; comic opera	*The Barber of Seville (Compact Classics: Vol. II/p. 35)*	Gioachino Rossini	H
17th century—England; Newfoundland; piracy	*The Dark Frigate*	Charles Boardman Hawes	M H
17th century—Salem, MA; witch hunts	*The Crucible*	Arthur Miller	M H
1604–1611—English translation of the Bible	*The King's Book*	Louise A. Vernon	E
1605–1691—Parisian monastery	*The Practice of the Presence of God*	Brother Lawrence	M H
1605–1691—Nicholas Herman of France 1884–1970—United States	*Practicing His Presence*	Brother Lawrence and Frank Laubach	M H

A clear and innocent conscience fears nothing.
—Queen Elizabeth I of England

Description or Time Period	Title	Author	Level
1605 and 1615—Former Spanish military hero writes the first modern novel to reflect on the meaning of human existence.	*Don Quixote of La Mancha, The Ingenious Gentleman (Compact Classics: Vol. I/5-D4)*	Miguel de Cervantes	M H
1606—Great Britain authorized explorers to establish colonies in The New World.	*First Charter of Virginia*	King James I	H
1607—The New World; Captain John Smith	*Blood on the River: Jamestown 1607*	Elisa Carbone	E
1607—Virginia	*Pocahontas*	Edgar and Parin D'Aulaire	E
1607—Jamestown, Virginia	*Three Ships Come Sailing*	Gilchrist Waring	E M
1607—Jamestown, Virginia	*Pocahontas and the Strangers*	Clyde Robert Bulla	E M
1609–1834—founding of Santa Fe, NM	*Tree in the Trail*	Holling Clancy Holling	E M
1609—London; Virginia Colony	*A Lion to Guard Us*	Clyde Robert Bulla	E M
1611—England; influenced the development of the English-speaking world	*King James Version of the Holy Bible*	commissioned by King James I	E M H
the story of immigration	*Coming to America*	Betsy Maestro	E
1600s—Holland; Pilgrims; Plymouth; pirates	*Salt in His Blood*	William R. Rang	E M
1600s—Irish physician; slavery; piracy	*Captain Blood* (based on novel by Rafael Sabatini)	1935 film starring Errol Flynn	H
1613–1667—writing of an English Anglican priest	*Rule and Exercises of Holy Living*	Jeremy Taylor	H
1618–1648—Scotland and Europe; the Thirty Years War	*The Lion of the North* (audio storytelling recording)	Jim Weiss http://greathall.com	E M H
1620–1627—England, Holland, Atlantic, and Massachusetts; Gov. Bradford's personal record	*Of Plymouth Plantation*	William Bradford	E M H
1620—Pilgrims; Mayflower	*The Thanksgiving Story*	Alice Dalgliesh	E M
1620–1621—Pilgrims found Plimoth Colony.	*The Pilgrims of Plimoth*	Marcia Sewall	E M
1620—from the History of Plymouth Plantation	*The Mayflower Compact*	William Bradford	H
1620—England to Massachusetts	*If You Sailed on the Mayflower in 1620*	Ann McGovern	E
1620s—Plymouth Colony, New England	*The First Thanksgiving*	Jean Craighead George	E
1620s—Plymouth Colony, New England	*Squanto, Friend of the Pilgrims*	Clyde Robert Bulla	E M
1620–1623—England, Holland, and Massachusetts	*The Landing of the Pilgrims*	James Daugherty	E M H

That Shakespeare was a typical man of the Renaissance is clear from his zest, his boldness, his humor, his love of beauty, and his incisive faith in the enterprise of living. This appears nowhere more obviously than in the sources of his plays, for these sources were to him records of various things that had happened to men and women under the will and providence of God.

—Hardin Craig, *An Introduction to Shakespeare*

Description or Time Period	Title	Author	Level
1620—English politician and scientist begins dismantling the Christian classical tradition through empirical science.	*The New Organon*	Francis Bacon	H
1620—Mayflower; New World—story of one of the surviving 102 passengers	*Almost Home*	Wendy Lawton	E
1620—Mayflower; New World	*Voyage to Freedom*	David Gay	E M
1620–1623—England; Holland; Massachusetts	*The Landing of the Pilgrims*	James Daugherty	E M
1621—Plymouth Colony, New England	*Squanto and the First Thanksgiving*	Joyce Kessel	E
1621—Plymouth, Massachusetts	*The Courtship of Miles Standish (Compact Classics: Vol. I/5-J1)*	Henry Wadsworth Longfellow	H
1623–1662—French scientist and mathematician	*A Piece of the Mountain: The Story of Blaise Pascal*	Joyce McPherson	E
1628–1688—Puritan England; illustrated edition	*Dangerous Journey: The Story of Pilgrim's Progress*	Oliver Hunkin	E M H
1637—autobiography; philosopher challenges natural law with rational thought setting a new foundation for human knowledge	*Discourse on Method*	Rene Descartes	H
Western philosophical tradition	*Meditations on First Philosophy (Compact Classics: Vol. II/p. 379)*	Rene Descartes	H
1640s—Boston, Massachusetts; Puritan picture of guilt and grace	*The Scarlet Letter* (written in 1850) *(Compact Classics: Vol. I/5-A1)*	Nathaniel Hawthorne	H
1642–1727—conversion of physics into a mathematical system	*The Principia*	Isaac Newton Andrew Motte, translator	H
1642–1727—England	*Isaac Newton: "Solitary Scholar" (Compact Classics: Vol. I/4-A2)*	Biography: Pioneers in Science	M H
1642–1727—England	*Newton's Gift: How Sir Isaac Newton Unlocked the System of the World*	David Berlinski	H
1642–1651—English philosopher outlines political theory: social contract	*Leviathan: The Matter, Form and Power of a Commonwealth, Ecclesiastical and Civil (Compact Classics: Vol. II/p. 391)*	Thomas Hobbes	H
1643–1727—England; Calculus; gravity; motion	*The Ocean of Truth: The Story of Sir Isaac Newton*	Joyce McPherson	E
1643–1727—scientific history	*The Story of Science: Newton at the Center*	Joy Hakim	M H
1647—Westminster Abbey; advice on issues of worship, doctrine, government, and the discipline of the Church of England as requested by English parliament	*The Westminster Standards* (doctrine of God and duty of men) The Confession of Faith The Larger Catechism The Shorter Catechism	Westminster Assembly	M H

He who loses wealth loses much; he who loses a friend loses more; but he who loses courage loses all.

—Miguel de Cervantes

Description or Time Period	Title	Author	Level
1650—Massachusetts Bay Colony; bond servant	*The Iron Peacock*	Mary Stetson Clarke	E M
1651—English political philosopher; influenced by Descartes; began the dismantling of Classical natural law and traditional Christian theology	*Leviathan*	Thomas Hobbes	H
1665—London; the Great Plague	*Master Cornhill*	Eloise Jarvis McGraw	E M
1667—English epic of the fall of man; good vs. evil	*Paradise Lost (Compact Classics: Vol. I/5-B1)*	John Milton Scott Elledge, editor	H
1667—cosmic struggle of God and Satan across Heaven, Hell, and Earth following the Fall of Man	*Paradise Lost* (2009 unabridged audio recording by Tantor Media)	John Milton read by Simon Vance http://tantor.com	H
1670—French mathematician and inventor; defense of the Christian faith at the dawn of the scientific age; ponderings of the human condition	*Pensees*	Blaise Pascal	H
1670—Dutch philosopher; father of pantheism	*Treatise on Religious and Political Philosophy*	Benedict Spinoza	H
17th century—Scotland; colonial America	*Duncan's War*	Douglas Bond	E
17th century—Scottish Covenanters	*King's Arrow* (sequel to *Duncan's War*)	Douglas Bond	E
17th century—Scotland	*Rebel's Keep* (sequel to *King's Arrow*)	Douglas Bond	E
17th century puritans in Holland; William Brewster	*Stink Alley*	Jamie Gilson	M H
17th century—England	*Galileo and the Stargazers: Newton* (audio storytelling recording)	Jim Weiss http://greathall.com	E M H
1678—*A Pilgrim's Progress* published	*Dangerous Journey* (illustrated edition of *A Pilgrim's Progress)*	John Bunyan	E M H
1678—timeless religious allegory of one's journey from the City of Destruction to the Celestial City	*The Pilgrim's Progress (Compact Classics: Vol. III/p. 15)*	John Bunyan	H
simplified vocabulary and concepts	*Little Pilgrim's Progress* (from John Bunyan's classic)	Helen L. Taylor	E M
17th century England; blind daughter of John Bunyan	*The Tinker's Daughter: Based on the Life of Mary Bunyan*	Wendy Lawton	E M
17th century—France; Huguenot children	*The Escape* (prequel to *The Secret Mission)*	A. Van der Jagt	E

We, whose names are underwritten, the loyal subjects of our dread sovereigne Lord, King James, by the grace of God, of Great Britaine, France, and Ireland king, defender of the faith, etc., having undertaken, for the glory of God, and advancement of the Christian faith, and honour of our king and country, a voyage to plant the first colony in the Northerne parts of Virginia ...

—The Mayflower Compact, 1620

Description or Time Period	Title	Author	Level
17th century—France; Huguenot persecution	*The Secret Mission* (sequel to *The Escape*)	A. Van der Jagt	E
1685—Huguenot life in La Rochelle, France	*Huguenot Garden*	Douglas M. Jones, III	E
1685—Russian tsar	*Peter the Great*	Diane Stanley	E
1685–1759—George Friedrich Handel	*The Handel's Messiah Family Advent Reader*	Donna W. Payne and Frances Lenzo	E M H
1686—French persecution of Huguenots	*Escape Across the Wide Sea*	Katherine Kirkpatrick	E M
1687—Connecticut puritans	*The Witch of Blackbird Pond* *(Compact Classics: Vol. II/p. 101)*	Elizabeth George Speare	M
1690—social contract incorporating traditional natural law; goodness of people	*Two Treatises of Government*	John Locke	H
1690—English philosopher	*An Essay Concerning Human Understanding* *(Compact Classics: Vol. II/p. 383)*	John Locke	H
1692—Salem Village, Massachusetts	*The Witchcraft of Salem Village*	Shirley Jackson	E M
1693—Boston, Massachusetts—sermons, conditions of the colony, and witch trials in Europe	*Wonders of the Invisible World*	Cotton Mather	H
Literature; Western Culture since the Reformation	*The Norton Anthology of World Masterpieces—Volume 2*	Maynard Mack, general editor	H
1600s or 1700s—Europe	*The Whipping Boy*	Sid Fleischman	E
1600s—Renaissance Italy	*Three Musketeers* (audio storytelling recording)	Jim Weiss http://greathall.com	E M H
1700s—France; musketeers	*The Man in the Iron Mask*	Alexandre Dumas	H
1700s—France	*The Three Musketeers* (based on book by Alexandre Dumas)	1948 film starring Gene Kelly	E M H
1700s—Europe	*The Scarlet Pimpernel*	Baroness Orczy	H
1700s—England, Hispaniola, and Treasure Island	*Treasure Island (Compact Classics: Vol. II/p. 121)*	Robert Louis Stevenson	M H
1700s—England, Hispaniola, and Treasure Island	*Treasure Island* (audio storytelling recording)	adapted and retold by Jim Weiss http://greathall.com	E M H

Henceforth I learn that to obey is best,
And love with fear the only God, to walk
As in his presence, ever to observe
His providence, and on him sole depend,
Merciful over all his works, with good
Still overcoming evil.

—John Milton, *Paradise Lost*

Description or Time Period	Title	Author	Level
1700s—England, Hispaniola, and Treasure Island	*Treasure Island*	1950 film shot in England	M H
1700s—America	*America's Godly Heritage* (documentary)	http://wallbuilders.com	M H
1700s—America	*Education and the Founding Fathers* (documentary)	http://wallbuilders.com	M H
1703–1791—England	*Sermons*	John Wesley	E M H
1703–1791—England	*A Heart Strangely Warmed: The Life of John Wesley*	Louise A. Vernon	M H
1706–1757—scientist, inventor, writer, and politician	*Benjamin Franklin: The Autobiography and Other Writings*	Benjamin Franklin	M H
1706–1757—Boston	*Benjamin Franklin: "America's Renaissance Man" (Compact Classics: Vol. I/4 B2)*	Biography: Leaders in Crisis	M H
1707–1788—England	*Hymns*	Charles Wesley	E M H
early 1700s—before horses	*Om-Kas-Toe: Blackfoot Twin Captures an Elkdog*	Kenneth Thomasma	E M
1707—Connecticut; true story	*The Courage of Sarah Noble*	Alice Dalgliesh	E M
1715—Scottish highlands during the time of the Jacobite Rising	*Rob Roy*	Sir Walter Scott	M H
1718–1747—missionary to American Indians in NY, NJ, and PA	*The Life and Diary of David Brainerd*	published by Jonathan Edwards	H
1719—Scottish castaway on Pacific island	*Robinson Crusoe (Compact Classics: Vol. I/5-E5)*	Daniel Defoe	M H
1725—New England; African prince; slavery	*Amos Fortune, Free Man* (based on a true story)	Elizabeth Yates	E M H
1720–1772—Northampton, NJ; autobiography of minister to Indians; anti-slavery in America	*The Journal of John Woolman*	John Woolman	H
1726—Anglo-Irish clergyman depicts the blindness of pride through satire	*Gulliver's Travels*	Jonathan Swift	M H
1726—Anglo-Irish clergyman depicts the blindness of pride through satire	*Gulliver's Travels* (audio storytelling recording)	adapted and retold by Jim Weiss http://greathall.com	E M H
1728–1779—British navigator and cartographer	*Captain Cook's Explorations*	James Cook	H
1728–1779—British Royal Navy	*Stowaway: The Story of Captain James Cook*	Karen Hesse	E M
America's legal model explained	*Whatever Happened to Justice?*	Richard J. Maybury	H
1732–1799—man, general, and first US President	*George Washington: A Biography*	Washington Irving	H
1732–1799—VA, MA, and NY	*George Washington*	Ingri and Edgar Parin D'Aulaire	E

Well, Faithful, thou hast faithfully profest unto thy Lord: with whom thou shalt be blest;
When faithless ones, with all their vain delights, are crying out under their hellish plights,
Sing, Faithful, sing; and let thy name survive, for though they kill'd thee, thou art yet alive.

—John Bunyan, *The Pilgrim's Progress*

Description or Time Period	Title	Author	Level
1732–1799—Virginia	*George Washington—A Picture Book Biography*	James Cross Giblin	E M
1732–1799—Virginia	*If You Grew Up with George Washington*	Ruth Belov Gross	E
1732–1799—Virginia	*George Washington—Soldier, Hero, President*	Justine Korman and Ron Fontes	E
1730s—Philadelphia	*Ben Franklin of Old Philadelphia*	Margaret Cousins	E M
1732–1799—Virginia	*Meet George Washington*	Joan Heilbroner	E M
1732–1799—Virginia	*George Washington: "American Patriot-Leader" (Compact Classics: Vol. I/4-B4)*	Biography: Leaders in Crisis	M H
1732–1799—man, general, president; against whom all others are judged	*Being George Washington: The Indispensable Man, as You've Never Seen Him*	Glenn Beck	H
1732–1799—Franklin, Voltaire, Napoleon, etc.	*George Washington's World*	Genevieve Foster	E M H
1735–1791—American Revolution	*A History of US (3) From Colonies to Country*	Joy Hakim	M H
1735–1826—Boston; American Founding Father, lawyer, statesman, diplomat, and 2nd US president	*Diary and Autobiography of John Adams*	John Adams L. Butterfield, editor	H
1736–1799—Virginia	*Give Me Liberty: The Christian Patriotism of Patrick Henry*	David Vaughan	H
1738–1820—England; biography; King George III	*Can't You Make Them Behave, King George?*	Jean Fritz	E M
1739—Christmas carol disallowed by English Puritan parliament	"Hark! The Herald Angels Sing" (1840—tune by Felix Mendelssohn)	Charles Wesley	E M H
1740—colonial New York	*The Deerslayer (Compact Classics: Vol. III/p. 149)*	James Fenimore Cooper	H
1743–1826—Virginia	*Meet Thomas Jefferson*	Marvin Barrett	E M
1743–1826—Virginia	*Thomas Jefferson "Quiet Author of Ideas" (Compact Classics: Vol. I/4-B5)*	Biography: Leaders in Crisis	H
1743–1826—Virginia	*Thomas Jefferson*	film by Ken Burns	M H
1743–1794—Paris, France	*Antoine Lavoisier: "Founder of Modern Chemistry" (Compact Classics: Vol. I/4-D5)*	Biography: Inventors and Innovators	M H
1743—the New World	*Calico Bush*	Rachel Field	E M

Contrary to contemporary, popular belief, some things do stand the test of time. In fact, not only do they stand, but they actually become dearer because of surviving the ages. ... Messiah has been performed somewhere in the world every year since its debut in 1742. ... Hallelujah! For the Lord God Omnipotent reigneth. The kingdom of this world is become the kingdom of our Lord and of His Christ; and He shall reign for ever and ever, King of Kings, and Lord of Lords. Hallelujah!

—Donna W. Payne, *The Handel's Messiah Family Advent Reader*

Description or Time Period	Title	Author	Level
1746—New England revivalist preaches the profound greatness of God.	*A Treatise Concerning Religious Affections*	Jonathan Edwards	H
1747–1798—Vermont	*Justin Morgan Had a Horse*	Marguerite Henry	E M
1748—Secular Scottish philosopher argues against social contract based on natural law.	*Of the Original Contract*	David Hume	H
1750—Germany to America	*The Skippack School*	Marguerite de Angeli	E M
1750s—Shawnee raid on settlers; true story	*Follow the River* (based on book by James A. Thorn)	1995 film	H
1751–1836—politician, philosopher and president	*The Great Little Madison*	Jean Fritz	E M
1752—Philadelphia, PA	*What's the Big Idea, Ben Franklin?*	Jean Fritz	E M
1756–1763—French and Indian War	*Struggle for a Continent: The French and Indian War*	Betsy and Giulio Maestro	M H
1754—Charlestown, NH; Indian raid; kidnapping	*Calico Captive* (based on the true story of Susanna W. Johnson)	Elizabeth George Speare	M
1756–1763—Fort Duquesne, Fort Necessity, Fort Ticonderoga and Fort William Henry	*With Wolfe in Canada: A Tale of the French and Indian Wars*	G. A. Henty	M H
1756–1763—Fort Duquesne, Fort Necessity, Fort Ticonderoga and Fort William Henry	*With Wolfe in Canada: A Tale of the French and Indian Wars* (unabridged audio book)	Jim Hodges http://jimhodgesaudiobooks.com	E M H
1757—Upper NY; French and Indian Wars	*The Last of the Mohicans*	1936 film starring Randolph Scott	H
1757—Upper New York; French and Indian Wars; British vs. Colonial settlers	*The Last of the Mohicans* *(Compact Classics: Vol. I/5-C5)*	James Fenimore Cooper	H
1757—Albany, NY; French and Indian wars	*The Matchlock Gun*	Walter D. Edmonds	E M
1758–1834—Continental Army	*Why Not, Lafayette?*	Jean Fritz	E M H
1758—eastern PA, OH, and NY	*Indian Captive: The Story of Mary Jemison*	Lois Lenski	M H
1759—An Englishman reflects on Christian morals and the regulation of common life.	*Rasselas and Essays*	Samuel Johnson	H
1760–1820—reign during American revolution	*Can't You Make Them Behave, King George?*	Jean Fritz	E
1760s—Pittsburgh; settlers vs. Redcoats	*Allegheny Uprising* (based on true story)	1939 film starring John Wayne	H
1761–1834—England, India; pioneer missionary	*William Carey: Obliged to Go*	Janet and Geoff Benge	E M
1762—Swiss political philosopher influenced the French Revolution with secular psychology-centered modernistic thought.	*The Social Contract* *(Compact Classics: Vol. II/p. 393)*	Jean-Jacques Rousseau	H

That night Sarah slept warm under the quilts. On a peg nearby hung her cloak—and she did not need it. She had kept up her courage and it was something that would be always with her. Always—even when the cloak was all worn out.

—Alice Dalgliesh, *The Courage of Sarah Noble*

Description or Time Period	Title	Author	Level
1763–1783—Massachusetts	*Liberty or Death: The American Revolution*	Betsy and Giulio Maestro	E
compare and contrast English, American, French and Russian revolutions	*The Revolutionary Age—Part 3 (World Views of the Western World)*	David Quine http://cornerstonecurriculum.com	H
War for Independence—American POW	*The Reb and the Redcoats*	Constance Savery	M H
1763—Maine wilderness	*The Sign of the Beaver*	Elizabeth George Speare	E M
1763–1815—America newly formed	*The New Republic: A Primary Source History of the U. S.*	George E. Stanley	H
1765—reaction to British encroachment upon rights through the Stamp Act	*Declaration of Rights*	Delegates from Nine American Colonies	H
1768–1772—tour of the colonies	*Squalls Before War: His Majesty's Schooner Sultana*	Ned Bustard	E M
1769–1794—Austria and France	*Marie Antoinette: Princess of Versailles*	Kathryn Lasky	M H
1769–1818—Kentucky	*Daniel Boone: His Own Story*	Daniel Boone, F. L. Hawks	M H
American Revolution	*Heroes of the Revolution*	David A. Adler	E M
Christian and Biblical roots for America	*Never Before in History: America's Inspired Birth*	Gary Amos and Richard Gardiner	H
1773—Boston; Revolutionary War	*Johnny Tremain*	Esther Forbes	E M
1774–1781—English perspective on the American Revolution	*True to the Old Flag: A Tale of the American War of Independence*	G. A. Henty	M H
1774–1781—English perspective on the American Revolution	*True to the Old Flag: A Tale of the American War of Independence* (unabridged audio book)	Jim Hodges http://jimhodgesaudiobooks.com	E M H
1775–1783—Massachusetts	*George the Drummer Boy*	Nathaniel Benchley	E
1775—Massachusetts	*Early Thunder*	Jean Fritz	E M H
Revolutionary War	*American Revolution Battles and Leaders*	Dorling Kindersley	E M
Revolutionary War	*Toliver's Secret*	Esther Wood Brady	E M
1775–1783—upper NY; Mohawk valley; American Revolution	*Drums Along the Mohawk (Compact Classics: Vol. II/p. 117)*	Walter Edmonds	M H
1775–1783—American Revolution	*Katie's Trunk*	Ann Turner	E

On October 9 he touched off the first cannon and the bombardment of Yorktown began. After ten days Cornwallis raised the white flag of surrender. That afternoon the British troops in their red uniforms marched slowly out of Yorktown while their bands played a popular English tune, "The World Upside Down." The British troops passed between lines of French and American troops who stood in respectful silence in obedience to Washington's command.

—Genevieve Foster, *George Washington's World*

Description or Time Period	Title	Author	Level
1775—patriot of the American Revolution	*And Then What Happened, Paul Revere?*	Jean Fritz	E M
1775—Massachusetts; Lexington and Concord	*Sam the Minuteman*	Nathaniel Benchley	E
1775—CT family split over war and politics	*My Brother Sam Is Dead*	James Lincoln Collier	M
1775—the great cannon trek	*Guns for General Washington*	Seymour Reit	E M
1775—Virginia; founding father	*Where Was Patrick Henry on the 29th of May?*	Jean Fritz	E M
1775—American Revolution	*What You Should Know About The American Flag*	Earl P. Williams, Jr.	M
1775—rulers and their times	*Louis XVI, Marie-Antoinette and the French Revolution*	Nancy Plain	M H
1776—Scottish social philosopher of the Enlightenment; theory of economic sciences; human progress through scientific knowledge	*An Inquiry Into the Nature and Causes of The Wealth of Nations (Compact Classics: Vol. II/p. 405)*	Adam Smith	H
1776—George Washington's housekeeper	*Phoebe the Spy*	Judith B. Griffin	E M
1776—Philadelphia—Second Continental Congress declared the United Colonies independent from the British Crown.	The Declaration of Independence	Committee—2nd Continental Congress: Jefferson, Adams, Sherman and Livingstone	E M H
1776—Independence Hall; Philadelphia, PA	*If You Were There When They Signed the Constitution*	Elizabeth Levy	M H
1776—Pennsylvania; first document requesting independence from Britain	*Common Sense*	Thomas Paine	M H
1776—1802	*The Oxford History of the French Revolution*	William Doyle	M
1777—2nd Continental Congress	Articles of Confederation	Committee—Continental Congress	H
1777–1778—Continental Army at Valley Forge	*The Winter at Valley Forge*	James E. Knight	E M
1777—America	*What You Should Know About The American Flag*	Earl P. Williams	E M H
1777—England; pacifist Quaker; Indian scout	*The Arrow Over the Door*	Joseph Bruchac and James Watling	E
1778—1784—Setauket spy ring	*Redcoats and Petticoats*	Katherine Kirkpatrick	E
1778—initiated the introspective, self-absorbed psychology-centered modern world	*Confessions* (autobiography)	Jean-Jacques Rousseau	H

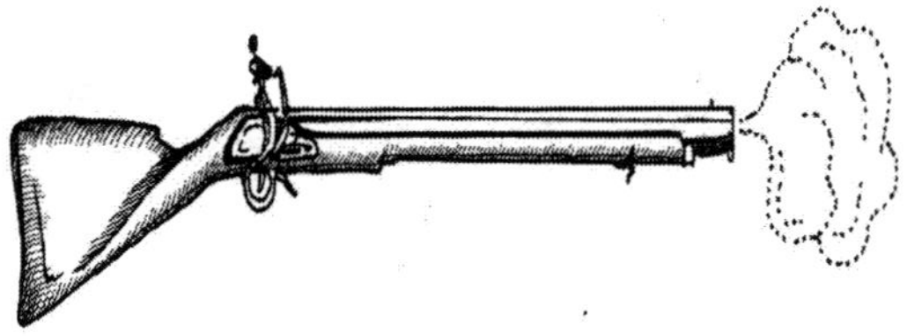

Now, walking up to the garden patch, across the wind, she wondered whether she had not been acting hysterically. She had put Edward under a strain that no boy only ten years old ought to have. She had left him frightened, cold, with his resolution to be brave. She seemed to see him sitting there by the table at the end of the monstrous gun, listening and listening. But she knew that she could have done nothing else.

—Walter D. Edmonds, *The Matchlock Gun*

Description or Time Period	Title	Author	Level
1779–1843—Fort McHenry, Maryland	*Francis Scott Key: God's Courageous Composer*	David Collins	M H
1780—defector from Continental to British army	*Traitor: The Case of Benedict Arnold*	Jean Fritz	M
1781—German modern philosopher of the Enlightenment; introduced the secular natural order—metaphysics	*Critique of Pure Reason* *(Compact Classics: Vol. II/p. 387)*	Immanuel Kant	H
late 18th century—abolition of slave trade in Great Britain	*Amazing Grace*—William Wilberforce	2006 film starring Ioan Gruffudd	E M H
late 18th century—abolition of slave trade in Great Britain	*William Wilberforce*	John Holzmann	E
late 18th century—fight to abolish slave trade	*The Kidnapped Prince: The Life of Olaudah Equiano*	Ann Cameron	E
1783—complete independence from Great Britain following surrender of Cornwallis	*Treaty With Great Britain*	Franklin, Adams, Jay and Laurens	H
1784—Pennsylvania frontier	*The Cabin Faced West*	Jean Fritz	E M H
1785—Europe's national anthem	"Ode to Joy" (from Beethoven's Symphony No. 9)	Friedrich Schiller	M H
1785—Germany	*Grimm's Fairy Tales*	Jacob and Wilhelm Grimm	E M H
1785—Germany	*Cinderella*	illustrated by Otto S. Svend	E M H
1786–1836—American hero	*Davy Crockett: His Own Story* (1834 autobiography)	David Crockett	M
1786–1836—backwoods TN; hero at the Alamo	*Life of David Crockett*	David Crockett	M H
1786–1836—backwoods TN; hero at the Alamo	*Davy Crockett: King of the Wild Frontier*	1955 film starring Fess Parker	E M H
1787–1788—85 letters published in NY newspapers to help ratify proposed U.S. Constitution	*The Federalist Papers*	Alexander Hamilton, James Madison, John Jay	H
1787—replaced the Articles of Confederation for the governance of the U.S.	The Constitution of the United States	Thomas Jefferson	E M H
1787–1790—United States	*Shh! We're Writing the Constitution*	Jean Fritz	E M
1788–1850—Burma, SE Asia; Adoniram Judson	*Imprisoned in the Golden City*	Dave, Neta, and Julian Jackson	E M
atoms, molecules, and chemical reactions	*The Usborne Introduction: Chemistry*	Usborne	H

I'll tell him to watch the spire of Christ's Church. You can see it well from Charlestown. If the British go out over the Neck, we will show one lantern. If in the boats—two.

—Esther Forbes, *Johnny Tremain*

The liberties of our country, the freedom of our civil Constitution, are worth defending at all hazards; and it is our duty to defend them against all attacks.

—Samuel Adams

Description or Time Period	Title	Author	Level
1789—English philosopher; legal and social reformer	*Introduction to the Principles of Morals and Legislation*	Jeremy Bentham	H
1789–1850—America	*A History of US (4) The New Nation*	Joy Hakim	E M H
1789–1799—terror and suffering during the French Revolution; London and Paris	*A Tale of Two Cities (Compact Classics: Vol. I/5-C1)*	Charles Dickens	H
1789–1799—London and Paris during the French Revolution	*A Tale of Two Cities* (audio storytelling recording)	adapted and retold by Jim Weiss http://greathall.com	E M H
1789–1799—the French Revolution	*In the Reign of Terror: An English Lad in the French Revolution*	G. A. Henty	M H
1789–1799—the French Revolution	*In the Reign of Terror: An English Lad in the French Revolution* audio book	Jim Hodges http://jimhodgesaudiobooks.com	E M H
1789–1799—French Revolution	*Stone Soup*	Marcia Brown	E
1789–1799—French Revolution	*In Search of Honor*	Donna Lynn Hess	E M
French Revolution—twin brothers separated at birth; corrupt King of France	*Man in the Iron Mask* (1934 and 1977 film versions based on the novel)	Alexandre Dumas	H
French Revolution	*The Scarlet Pimpernel* (1982 film version with Jane Seymour)	Baroness Orczy	H
1789—south sea voyage	*Mutiny on the Bounty*	Charles Nordhoff	M H
1789—south sea voyage	*Mutiny on the Bounty*	1935 film starring Clark Gable	M H
1790—British political activist	*Reflections on the Revolution in France*	Edmund Burke	H
1790–1832—France and Egypt	*Seeker of Knowledge: The Man Who Deciphered Egyptian Hieroglyphics*	James Rumford	E
1791	*The Rights of Man*	Thomas Paine	H
1791–1867—English chemist invented electric motor, transformer, and generator.	*Michael Faraday: Father of Electronics*	Charles Ludwig	M H
1791—biography by Scottish friend	*The Life of Samuel Johnson, LL.D*	James Boswell	H

Along the Paris streets, the death carts rumble, hollow and harsh .... All the devouring and insatiate monsters imagined since imagination could record itself, are fused in the one realization, Guillotine .... Crush humanity out of shape once more, under similar hammers, and it will twist itself into the same tortured forms. Sow the same seed of rapacious license and oppression over again, and it will surely yield the same fruit according to its kind.

—Charles Dickens, *A Tale of Two Cities*

Description or Time Period	Title	Author	Level
18th century Japan	*The Master Puppeteer*	Katherine Paterson	E
Post-Revolution; Massachusetts—true story	*Carry On, Mr. Bowditch* (unabridged audio version by Jim Weiss)	Jean Lee Latham http://greathall.com	E M
Revolutionary War tale	*The Legend of Sleepy Hollow* and *Rip Van Winkle*	Washington Irving	M
late 1700s—United States	*Rip Van Winkle* (audio storytelling recording)	adapted and retold by Jim Weiss http://greathall.com	E M H
1792–1797—SW England	*Sense and Sensibility (Compact Classics: Vol. II/p. 123)*	Jane Austen	H
1792–1797—SW England	*Sense and Sensibility* (based on the book by Jane Austen)	1995 film starring Emma Thompson and Alan Rickman	H
1793—American South	*The Story of Eli Whitney*	Jean Lee Latham	E M
1793–1863—Texas	*Raven: A Biography of Sam Houston*	Marquis James	H
1793—Paris; rural France; French Revolution	*In the Reign of Terror*	G. A. Henty	M H
1793—Paris; rural France; French Revolution	*In the Reign of Terror* (audio storytelling recording)	Jim Weiss http://greathall.com	E M H
1794–1858—opening of Japan; U.S. Navy	*Commodore Perry and the Land of the Shogun*	Rhoda Blumberg	E M H
late 1700s—Switzerland; science fiction horror novel	*Frankenstein (Compact Classics: Vol. I/5-F2)*	Mary Shelley	H
late 1700s—Switzerland; science fiction horror novel	*Frankenstein* (unabridged audio recording by Jim Weiss)	Mary Shelley	H
1796	Washington's Farewell Address	George Washington	H
1797—Philadelphia	*Abigail Adams—Witness to a Revolution*	Natalie Bober	M
1797—epic ballad of forgiveness	*The Rime of the Ancient Mariner (Compact Classics: Vol. I/5-D1)*	Samuel Taylor Coleridge	H
1798—English poetry	lyrical ballads	William Wordsworth Samuel Taylor Coleridge	H
1800s—northern England	*Jane Eyre (Compact Classics: Vol. I/5-J5)*	Charlotte Bronte	H
1800s—northern England	*Jane Eyre* (based on the book by Charlotte Bronte)	1997 film starring Samantha Morton	H

All these, however, were mere terrors of the night, phantoms of the mind that walk in darkness; and though he had seen many spectres in his time, and been more than once beset by Satan in divers shapes, in his lonely pre-ambulations, yet daylight put an end to all these evils; and he would have passed a pleasant life of it, in despite of the Devil and all his works, if his path had not been crossed by a being that causes more perplexity to mortal man than ghosts, goblins, and the whole race of witches put together, and that was—a woman.

—Washington Irving, *The Legend of Sleepy Hollow*

Description or Time Period	Title	Author	Level
19th century England; moral values	*Great Expectations* (written in 1860) *(Compact Classics: Vol. III/p. 153)*	Charles Dickens	H
19th century England; moral values	*Great Expectations* (based on the book by Charles Dickens)	1946 British film featuring Alec Guinness	M H
1800s—orphan and bedridden cousin	*The Secret Garden*	Frances Hodgson Burnett	M
1800s—orphan and bedridden cousin	*The Secret Garden* (based on the book by Frances Hodgson Burnett)	1993 film starring Kate Maberly	E M H
1800s—London, England	*A Christmas Carol* (written in 1843)	Charles Dickens	H
early 19th century—rural English village during the Industrial Revolution	*Silas Marner (Compact Classics: Vol. I/5-J3)*	George Eliot (Mary Ann Evans)	H
early 19th century British satire; worldliness	*Vanity Fair*	William Makepeace Thackeray	H
1800s—Colonial Africa	*Things Fall Apart*	Chinua Achebe	H
19th century colonial India	*The Jungle Book (Compact Classics: Vol. III/p. 3)*	Rudyard Kipling	M H
19th century colonial India	*The Jungle Book* (audio storytelling recording)	adapted and retold by Jim Weiss http://greathall.com	E M H
1800s—Japanese tsunami	*The Big Wave*	Pearl S. Buck	E
1800s—family shipwrecked; West Indies	*The Swiss Family Robinson*	Johann D. Wyss	E M H
1800s—family shipwrecked; West Indies	*The Swiss Family Robinson* (based on book by Johann D. Wyss)	1960 film with James MacArthur	E M H
1800s—frontier Ohio; late 1800s—England	*The Short Stories of G. A. Henty* (audio storytelling recording)	adapted and retold by Jim Weiss http://greathall.com	E M H
1803—Lewis and Clark expedition	*Streams to the River, River to the Sea*	Scott O'Dell	M H
1803–1851—gorgeous picture book	*Into the Woods: A James Audubon Book*	Robert Burleigh	E M
1803–1806—Louisiana purchase	*The Journals of Lewis and Clark*	Anthony Brandt	M H
1803–1806—Jefferson, Lewis, Clark and the opening of the American West	*Of Courage Undaunted*	James Daugherty	M H

First in war, first in peace, and first in the hearts of his countrymen, he was second to none in humble and enduring scenes of private life. Pious, just, humane, temperate, and sincere; uniform dignified, and commanding; his example was as edifying to all around him as were the effects of that example lasting correct throughout, vice shuddered in his presence and virtue always felt his fostering hand. The purity of his private charter gave effulgence to his public virtues. Such was the man for whom our nation mourns.

—Congressman Henry "Light-Horse Harry" Lee, official eulogy of George Washington, December 26, 1799

Description or Time Period	Title	Author	Level
1803–1806—Louisiana territory; original diaries and maps	*As Far as the Eye Can Reach: Lewis and Clark's Westward Quest*	Elizabeth Cody Kimmel	E M
1803–1806—Lewis and Clark expedition	*Seaman: Dog Who Explored the West with Lewis and Clark*	Gail Langer Karwoski	E M
1803–1806—Lewis and Clark expedition	*Seaman's Journal: On the Trail of Lewis and Clark*	Patti Reeder Eubank	E M
1803–1806—Louisiana territory	*Lewis and Clark: The Journey of the Corps of Discovery*	Film by Ken Burns, Dayton Duncan	M H
1803–1806—Lewis and Clark expedition	*The Lewis and Clark Expedition*	Richard Neuberger	E M
1803—Louisiana purchase by Thomas Jefferson; Lewis and Clark expedition	*Far Horizons*	1955 film starring Charlton Heston	M H
1803—agreement with Napoleon to purchase Louisiana territory	*Treaty with France: Louisiana Purchase*	Livingston, Monroe, and Marbois	M H
early 19th century—Tennessee frontier	*Davy Crockett, King of the Wild Frontier*	1955 series starring Fess Parker	E M H
1804—German retelling of Swiss folklore; William Tell shoots apple from his son's head.	*Legend of Wilhelm Tell: Hero of Switzerland*	Friedrich Schiller	M H
1805–1898—England; care of orphans	*George Muller of Bristol*	Arthur T. Pierson	H
1805–1875—Denmark	*Tales of Hans Christian Andersen*	translated by Naomi Lewis	E M
1805–1875—Denmark	*The Fairy Tale of My Life: An Autobiography*	Hans Christian Andersen	H
1805–1875—Denmark	*Fairy Tales by Hans Christian Andersen*	Hans Christian Andersen illustrated by Arthur Rackham	E M H
1807—Virginia	*A Picture Book of Robert E. Lee*	David A. Adler	E
1807–1870—Virginia	*Robert Edward Lee*	John J. Dwyer	M H
1807–1870—Virginia	*Virginia's General: Robert E. Lee and the Civil War*	Albert Marrin	H
1807–1870—Virginia; biography	*Robert E. Lee: Gallant Christian Soldier*	Lee Roddy	E M H
1807—invention of the steamboat	*Robert Fulton, Boy Craftsman*	Marguerite Henry	E M
1809–1852—France	*Louis Braille: The Boy Who Invented Books for the Blind*	Margaret Davidson	E M
1809–1865—overview of world history	*Abraham Lincoln's World*	Genevieve Foster	M H

Much more surprising things can happen to anyone who, when a disagreeable or discouraged thought comes into his mind, just has the sense to remember in time and push it out by putting in an agreeable, determinedly courageous one. Two things cannot be in one place.

—Frances Hodgson Burnett, *The Secret Garden*

Description or Time Period	Title	Author	Level
1809–1865—Lincoln's footsteps	*Lincoln: A Photobiography*	Russell Freedman	E M
1809–1865—Il, KY, and Washington, DC	*Abe Lincoln: Log Cabin to White House*	Sterling North	E M H
1809–1865—Kentucky	*Abraham Lincoln: "He Saved the Union"* *(Compact Classics: Vol. I/4-B3)*	Biography: Leaders in Crisis	M H
1809–1865—KY, IL, IN, and Washington DC	*Abraham Lincoln*	Ingri and Edgar Parin D'Aulaire	E
1809–1868—American Civil War	*Abraham Lincoln and the Heart of America* (audio storytelling recording)	Jim Weiss http://greathall.com	E M H
1809–1849—"The Tell-Tale Heart," "The Pit and the Pendulum," "The Cask of Amontillado"	*The Short Stories of Edgar Allan Poe* *(Compact Classics: Vol. II/p. 159)*	Edgar Allan Poe	H
1809–1849—Boston, Massachusetts; deeply melancholic detective fiction	*The Portable Poe*	Edgar Allan Poe	M H
1809–1849—Boston, Massachusetts	*The Poetry of Edgar Allan Poe* *(Compact Classics: Vol. II/p. 251)*	Edgar Allan Poe	M H
19th century English manor house; gothic horror story	*The Fall of the House of Usher* *(Compact Classics: Vol. I/5-F5)*	Edgar Allan Poe	H
1812—James Madison; war facts (videos)	*The War of 1812*	The History Channel	M H
1812—the Battle of New Orleans; story of Jean Lafitte and Andrew Jackson	*The Buccaneer*	1958 film starring Yul Brynner	M H
1812—Young Davy Crockett fights Creek Indians alongside Andrew Jackson.	*Rainbow in the Thunder*	1988 film starring Johnny Cash	M H
the Napoleonic era—Russia; historical account of French invasion of Russia	*War and Peace* *(Compact Classics: Vol. II/p. 227)*	Leo Tolstoy	H
the Napoleonic era—Russia; historical account of French invasion of Russia	*War and Peace*	1956 film starring Henry Fonda	H
1813—English novel; economic standing and personal virtue	*Pride and Prejudice (Compact Classics: Vol. I/5-L4)*	Jane Austen	H
1813—English novel; economic standing and personal virtue	*Price and Prejudice* (based on the book by Jane Austen)	2005 film starring Keira Knightley and Donald Sutherland	M H
1813–1952	*7 Men Who Rule the World from the Grave*	Dave Breese	H

There were once five and twenty tin soldiers. They were brothers, for they had all been made out of the same old tin spoon … Each was exactly like the rest to a hair, except one who had but one leg. He had been cast last of all, and there had not been quite enough tin to finish him. But he stood as firmly upon his one leg as the others upon their two, and it was he whose fortunes became so remarkable.

—Hans Christian Andersen, "The Steadfast Tin Soldier"

Description or Time Period	Title	Author	Level
1813–1874—Scottish missionary doctor explores central and southern Africa.	*How I Found Livingstone*	Sir Henry Morton Stanley	H
1813–1873—Africa; Scotland	*David Livingstone: African Explorer*	John Hudson Tiner	E M H
1813–1873—Scotland; S. Africa	*David Livingstone: Africa's Trailblazer*	Janet and Geoffe Benge	E M H
1813–1873—Reporter finds missionary in Africa.	*Stanley and Livingstone*	1939 film starring Spencer Tracy	M H
1815–1838—France; Italy; Mediterranean; hope, justice, vengeance, mercy, and forgiveness	*The Count of Monte Cristo*	Alexandre Dumas	H
1815–1838—France; Italy; Mediterranean; hope, justice, vengeance, mercy, and forgiveness	*The Count of Monte Cristo* (based on the book by Alexandre Dumas)	2002 film starring Jim Caviezel	H
1800s—costumes, ships, and warfare	*Horatio Hornblower*	1998 film starring Ioan Gruffudd	M H
1813—Underground Railroad	*Following Freedom's Star*	James Haskins and Kathleen Benson	M H
1814—Fort McHenry	*The Star-Spangled Banner*	Catherine A. Welch	E
1816—England	*Emma*	Jane Austen	H
1816—England	*Emma* (based on the book by Jane Austen)	1996 film starring Gwyneth Paltrow	H
1817—Influential German philosopher publishes ideas on dialectical logic.	*Logic (Compact Classics: Vol. II/p. 389)*	G.W.F. Hegel	H
1817—NY state; Lake Erie; Hudson River	*The Amazing Impossible Erie Canal*	Cheryl Harness	M H
1818—history of America at sea	*Seabird*	Holling Clancy Holling	E M
1819–1892—Long Island, NY	*Walt Whitman (Compact Classics: Vol. II/p.255)*	Biography	M H
1819—*The Legend of Sleepy Hollow* from *The Sketch Book*	*The Short Stories of Washington Irving (Compact Classics: Vol. III/p. 29)*	Washington Irving	H
1819—Young English poet relates on truth and life.	*The Great Odes*	John Keats	H
1820–1910—London	*Florence Nightingale: "Nursing's Founder" (Compact Classics: Vol. I/4-E3)*	Biography: Leaders of the Spirit	M H
1820–1860—America	*A History of US (5) Liberty for All?*	Joy Hakim	M H
1822–1885—Civil War	*Unconditional Surrender: U. S. Grant and the Civil War*	Albert Marrin	H

But, ere long, I felt myself getting pale and wishing them gone. My head ached, and I fancied a ringing in my ears; but still they sat and chatted. The ringing became more distinct: —It continued and became more distinct: I talked more freely to get rid of the feeling: but it continued and gained definiteness—until, at length, I found that the noise was not within my ears.

—Edgar Allan Poe, "The Tell-Tale Heart"

Description or Time Period	Title	Author	Level
1822–1895—France	*Louis Pasteur: Founder of Modern Medicine*	John Hudson Tiner	M H
1822–1895—Eastern France	*Louis Pasteur: "Chemist-Healer"* *(Compact Classics: Vol. I/4-D4)*	Biography: Inventors and Innovators	M H
1823—U.S. policy toward foreign powers	The Monroe Doctrine	James Monroe	M H
1824—German philosopher; ideology of nationalism	*Philosophy of History*	Georg Wilhelm Friedrich Hegel	H
1824–1863—Virginia	*Stonewall*	John J. Dwyer	H
1824–1863—Virginia	*Stonewall Jackson: Loved in the South, Admired in the North*	Charles Ludwig	E M H
1825—New York	*The Erie Canal*	R. Conrad Stein	E M
1828–1905—world travel	*Around the World in 80 Days*	Jules Verne	E M H
1828–1910—Russian novelist	*The Death of Ivan Ilyich*	Leo Tolstoy	H
1829–1909—Arizona; autobiography of Apache prisoner of war	*Geronimo: His Own Story* *(Compact Classics: Vol. III/p. 411)*	Geronimo	M H
1830–1832—New England	*A Gathering of Days*	Joan W. Blos	M H
1831—abolitionist newspaper	*The Liberator*	William Lloyd Garrison	H
1832—published	*McGuffey's Fourth Eclectic Reader*	William H. McGuffey	E M
1832—New Hampshire; colonial Boston	*Ox-Cart Man*	Donald Hall	E
1832–1898—England	*Alice's Adventures in Wonderland* and *Through the Looking-Glass*	Lewis Carroll (Charles Lutwidge Dodgson)	E M H
1832–1905—England; China	*God's Adventurer: Hudson Taylor*	Phyllis Thompson	E M H
1835—Pacific island	*Island of the Blue Dolphins* (based on a true story)	Scott O'Dell	E M
1835 published in Denmark	*Book of Fairy Tales*	Hans Christian Andersen	E
1835—observations of a Frenchman; American government	*Democracy in America*	Alexis de Tocqueville	H
1835—battle for Texas independence	*Lone Star*	1952 film starring Clark Gable	E M H
1835–1919—Scottish immigrant; made and gave away a vast American fortune	*The Autobiography of Andrew Carnegie* *(Compact Classics: Vol. III/p. 387)*	Andrew Carnegie	M H
1835–1910—Missouri; the story of Samuel Langhorne Clemens	*The Autobiography of Mark Twain* *(Compact Classics: Vol. III/p. 367)*	Mark Twain	M H

It is necessary to have wished for death in order to know how good it is to live.

—Alexandre Dumas, *The Count of Monte Cristo*

Description or Time Period	Title	Author	Level
1835–1842—Seminole wars in Florida	*Seminole*	1953 film starring Rock Hudson	M H
1836–1957—WI, MO, MN, IA, Dakota Territory	*Laura: The Life of Laura Ingalls Wilder*	Donald Zochert	E M H
writings by Laura Ingalls Wilder	*A Little House Reader*	edited by William Anderson	E M
1836—San Antonio, Texas	*Inside the Alamo*	Jim Murphy	M H
1836—San Antonio, Texas	*The Boy in the Alamo*	Margaret Cousins	M H
1837–1838—Appalachian Mountains; OK	*Soft Rain: A Story of the Cherokee Trail of Tears*	Cornelia Cornelissen	M H
1837–1838—Georgia to Arkansas	*Only the Names Remain: The Cherokees and the Trail of Tears*	Alex W. Bealer	M H
1838—Trail of Tears	*Sequoyah and the Cherokee Alphabet*	Robert Cwiklik	M H
1838—published; social injustices for English orphans	*Oliver Twist (Compact Classics: Vol. II/p. 141)*	Charles Dickens	M H
1838—published; social injustices for English orphans	*Oliver Twist* (based on book by Charles Dickens)	1948 film featuring Alec Guinness	M H
1839—Harvard	*The Poetry of Henry Wadsworth Longfellow (Compact Classics: Vol. II/p. 249)*	Henry Wadsworth Longfellow	M H
1840s—mid-America	*The Adventures of Tom Sawyer (Compact Classics: Vol. III/p. 121)*	Mark Twain	M H
1840s—mid-America	*The Adventures of Tom Sawyer* (audio storytelling recording)	adapted and retold by Jim Weiss http://greathall.com	E M H
1840s—mid-America	*The Adventures of Huckleberry Finn (Compact Classics: Vol. III/p. 123)*	Mark Twain	H
1840s—mid-America	*Life on the Mississippi*	Mark Twain	M H
Mississippi River	*Minn of the Mississippi*	Holling Clancy Holling	E M
Oregon Trail—Springfield, MO	The Lone Ranger	Radio classics	E M H
1840s—early California	*The Mark of Zorro*	1940 film starring Tyrone Power	M H
1840s—early California	*The Mask of Zorro*	1998 film with Anthony Hopkins	H
1840s—Oregon Trail	*Across the Wide and Lonesome Prairie*	Kristiana Gregory	E

But what then? What had he really gained by all this trouble? What had he brought back from this long and weary journey? Nothing, you say? Perhaps so; nothing but a charming woman, who, strange as it may appear, made him the happiest of men! Truly, would you not for less than that make the tour around the world?

—Jules Verne, *Around the World in 80 Days*

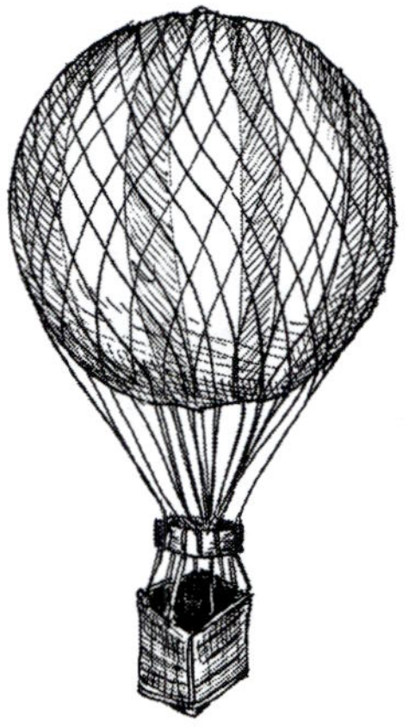

Description or Time Period	Title	Author	Level
1841–1844—American philosopher and developer of transcendentalism; America's intellectual Declaration of Independence	*The American Scholar*	Ralph Waldo Emerson	H
1844—Oregon Trail	*Stout-Hearted Seven: Orphaned on the Oregon Trail*	Neta Lohnes Frazier	E M
1844—telegraph	*Samuel F.B. Morse: Artist with a Message*	John Hudson Tiner	E M
1845—autobiography of an American slave	*Narrative of the Life of Frederick Douglass: An American Slave*	Frederick Douglass	H
1845–1847—Concord, Massachusetts; essays	"Walden" and "Civil Disobedience"	Henry David Thoreau	H
1846—Nebraska	*A Lantern in Her Hand*	Bess Streeter Aldrich	H
1846—Independence, MO	*The Journal of Douglas Allen Deeds: The Donner Party Expedition*	Rodman Philbrick	E M
1846—the Donner party	*Patty Reed's Doll*	Rachel K. Laurgaard	M
1847—U.K.—passion, betrayal, hatred, and death	*Wuthering Heights*	Emily Bronte	M H
1847—U.K.—passion, betrayal, hatred, and death	*Wuthering Heights* (based on the book by Emily Bronte)	1939 film with Laurence Olivier	H
1847–1922—Scotland	*Alexander Graham Bell—An Inventive Life*	Elizabeth MacLeod	M
1847–1922—Scotland	*Alexander Graham Bell—Inventor and Teacher*	Michael A. Schuman	M
1847–1922—Scotland; Bell's life story	*Alexander Graham Bell: The Sound and the Silence*	1992 film starring John Bach	M H
1847–1931—Ohio	*Thomas Edison: The Great American Inventor*	Louise Egan	M
1847–1931—New Jersey	*The Story of Thomas Alva Edison: Wizard of Menlo Park*	Margaret Davidson	H
1847–1931—New Jersey	*Thomas Alva Edison: "Blue-Collar Inventor" (Compact Classics: Vol. I/4-D1)*	Biography: Inventors and Innovators	M H
1848–1915—Scotland; Africa; missionary	*Mary Slessor: Forward to Calabar*	Janet Benge and Geoff Benge	E M H
Westward expansion—Arkansas—Oregon	*Bound for Oregon*	Jean Van Leeuwen	M H
Westward expansion—The Sager Family	*On to Oregon!*	Honore Morrow	M
Wagons travel West.	*Westward the Women*	1951 film starring Robert Taylor	E M H

"They belong to the old gentleman," said Oliver, wringing his hands; "to the good, kind, old gentleman who took me into his house, and had me nursed, when I was near dying of the fever. Oh, pray send them back; send him back the books and money .... He'll think I stole them; the old lady, all of them who were so kind to me, will think I stole them. Oh, do have mercy upon me, and send them back!"

—Charles Dickens, *Oliver Twist*

Description or Time Period	Title	Author	Level
1848—St. Joseph, MO	*Westward to Oregon*	Patricia Hermes	E M
1848—California gold rush	*The Secret Valley*	Clyde Robert Bulla	E
1848—Atheistic German philosopher views religion as an instrument of oppression and reveals the notion of scientific socialism.	*The Communist Manifesto (Compact Classics: Vol. II/p. 407)*	Karl Marx Friedrich Engels	H
1849—California gold rush	*By the Great Horn Spoon*	Eric von Schmidt	E M

Tom gave up the brush with reluctance in his face, but alacrity in his heart. And while the late steamer Big Missouri worked and sweated in the sun, the retired artist sat on a barrel in the shade close by, dangled his legs, munched his apple, and planned the slaughter of more innocents. There was no lack of material; boys happened along every little while; they came to jeer, but remained to whitewash.

—Mark Twain, *The Adventures of Tom Sawyer*

She kept me carefully in a box of relics in her bureau drawer. A lock of Grandma's hair wrapped in lace, a little knife and fork and spoon, and the tiny glass dish she had picked up that day when I fell out of her pocket on the desert—these all lay beside me on her father's big mitten, the one which had concealed the crumbs that had saved her life .... Someday she will be the sole survivor of the ill-fated Donner Party. Then she must go back to Sutter's Fort to tell the story of the children and their dolls who crossed the plains in '46.

—Rachel K. Laurgaard, *Patty Reed's Doll*

The Modern World

Timeline of Classics

Description or Time Period	Title	Author	Level
spiral-bound book of pages printed with a blank timeline; perfect for stickers, drawings, annotations, etc.	*The Timeline Book*	InquisiCorp Corporation http://sonlight.com	E M H
from Victoria's empire to the end of the USSR	*The Story of the World: Volume 4: The Modern Age*	Susan Wise Bauer http://peacehillpress.com	E M
from Victoria's empire to the end of the USSR	*The Story of the World: Volume 4: The Modern Age*	Unabridged reading by Jim Weiss http://greathall.com	E M
Western civilization from prehistoric man through the modern nation-state; as told by a grandfather to his grandchildren	*The Story of Mankind*	Hendrick Willem van Loon (updated by Gerrit van Loon and John M. Merriman)	E M
Western civilization from prehistoric man through the modern nation-state; as told by a grandfather to his grandchildren	*The Story of Mankind* (based on the book by Hendrick Willem van Loon)	1957 film adaptation featuring the Marx Brothers and Ronald Colman	H
literature of Western Culture since the Renaissance	*The Norton Anthology of World Masterpieces Vol. 2*	Maynard Mack, general editor	H
prehistoric to Post-Modern era	*The Annotated Mona Lisa: A Crash Course in Art History from Prehistoric to Post-Modern*	Carol Strickland	M H
fifty volumes of selected world classics from all main divisions of literature	*Fifteen Minutes a Day Reading Guide for The Harvard Classics (1909)*	Charles W. Eliot editor of *The Harvard Classics*	H
1492–2004—Columbus through War on Terror	*A Patriot's History of the United States*	Larry Schweikart and Michael Allen	H
1830s—Montana; cattlemen; Blackfoot territory	*The Big Sky*	A. B. Guthrie, Jr.	M H
1830s—development of Montana; cattlemen in Blackfoot territory	*The Big Sky* (based on the book by A. B. Guthrie)	1952 film starring Kirk Douglas	M H
1830—U.S. Frigate *Constitution*	*Old Ironsides*	Oliver Wendell Holmes	H
1835–1853—island rescue off California coast; inspired by true story	*Island of the Blue Dolphins (Compact Classics: Vol. III/p. 137)*	Scott O'Dell	E M H
1835, 1840—analysis of American government by a young French nobleman	*Democracy in America*	Alexis de Tocqueville	H
1835–1836—battle for Texas independence	*Lone Star*	1952 film starring Clark Gable	E M H
reminders of America's heritage—poems, speeches, quotes, songs, and profiles	*Patriot's Handbook*	George Grant	M H
from earliest times to the present; a large, detailed colorful fold-out resource	*The Wall Chart of World History*	Barnes & Noble, Inc.	E M H

An honest evaluation of the history of the United States must begin and end with the recognition that, compared to any other nation, America's past is a bright and shining light. America was, and is, the city on the hill, the fountain of hope, the beacon of liberty.

—Larry Schweikart and Michael Allen, *A Patriot's History of the United States*

Description or Time Period	Title	Author	Level
flow of history from 5000 BC to modern times in a table format that includes history and politics, literature and theater, religion and philosophy, visual arts and music, science and technology, and daily life	*The Timetables of History: A Horizontal Linkage of People and Events* (directly translated from *Kulturfahrplan: The Culture Timetables)*	Bernard Grun based on the work of Werner Stein and Wallace Brockway	E M H
1842—Paris, France	*The Hunchback of Notre Dame*	Victor Hugo	H
1843—Danish philosopher; founder of existential movement	*Fear and Trembling*	Soren Kierkegaard	H
1847—Ohio	*Young Tom Edison*	1940 film starring Mickey Rooney	E M H
1848—revised from *The Sketch Book;* first published in 1819—American gothic horror	*The Short Stories of Washington Irving (Compact Classics: Vol. III/p. 29)*	Washington Irving	H
1848—The Danish "Father of Modern Existentialism" discusses the corruption of human nature and sin.	*The Sickness Unto Death: A Christian Psychological Exposition (Compact Classics: Vol. II/p. 401)*	Soren Kierkegaard	H
1848—American essay against governmental interference and the rights of individuals	"On Civil Disobedience"	Henry David Thoreau	H
1848—German revolutionary secular atheistic socialist of the Enlightenment	*The Communist Manifesto*	Karl Marx	H
mid-19th century—analysis and criticism of capitalism; call for reform; communism	*Das Kapital (Compact Classics: Vol. I/5-K4)*	Karl Marx	H
1850–1894—London	*Dr. Jekyll and Mr. Hyde (Compact Classics: Vol. II/p. 163)*	Robert Louis Stevenson	H
1850–1866—Massachusetts	*The Complete Poems (Compact Classics: Vol. II/p. 257)*	Emily Dickinson	H
1850—guilt, grace, hypocrisy, and Puritan morality	*The Scarlet Letter*	Nathaniel Hawthorne	H
1850—UK—autobiographical social criticism	*David Copperfield*	Charles Dickens	H
1850—UK—autobiographical social criticism	*David Copperfield* (based on the book by Charles Dickens)	1935 film starring W. C. Fields and Lionel Barrymore	E M H
1850—San Francisco; purchase of Alaska	*World in His Arms*	1952 film starring Gregory Peck	M H
1850—NY—Cape Horn—CA	*Clipper Ship*	Thomas P. Lewis	E

Upon my arrival in the United States, the religious aspect of the country was the first thing that struck my attention; and the longer I stayed there, the more did I perceive the great political consequences resulting from this state of things, to which I was unaccustomed. In France I had almost always seen the spirit of religion and the spirit of freedom pursuing courses diametrically opposed to each other; but in America I found that they were intimately united, and that they reigned in common over the same country.

—Alexis de Tocqueville, *Democracy in America*

Description or Time Period	Title	Author	Level
1850—clipper ship, Cape Horn	*All Sail Set: A Romance of the Flying Cloud*	Armstrong Sperry	H
1850—Western United States	*The Josefina Story Quilt*	Eleanor Coerr	E
1851—SE United States	*The Drinking Gourd*	F. N. Monjo	E
1850s—Child born into slavery lives to participate in American civil rights movement.	*The Autobiography of Miss Jane Pittman*	Ernest J. Gaines	H
1818–1895—reformer, abolitionist	*Narrative of the Life of Frederick Douglass, An American Slave*	Frederick Douglass	H
1851—deeply theological novel	*Moby Dick (Compact Classics: Vol. I/5-D2)*	Herman Melville	H
1851—Deranged ship's captain seeks revenge.	*Moby Dick* (based on the book by Herman Melville)	1956 film starring Gregory Peck	H
Underground Railroad	*Freedom Train: The Story of Harriet Tubman*	Dorothy Sterling	H
Pre-Civil War—Kentucky; plight of slave families; abolition	*Uncle Tom's Cabin (Compact Classics: Vol. III/p.151)*	Harriet Beecher Stowe	H
1853—Commodore Perry opens Japan to U.S.	*Born in the Year of Courage*	Emily Crofford	E M H
1854—author's reflections on his life in MA woodlands	*Walden*	Henry David Thoreau	H
1855–1865—American Civil War	*A History of US (6) War, Terrible War*	Joy Hakim	M H
1809–1865—American President	*Lincoln: A Photobiography*	Russell Freedman	E M
1809–1865—American President	*Abraham Lincoln: A Photographic Story of a Life*	Tanya Lee Stone	E M
1855—the nature of humanity	*Leaves of Grass*	Walt Whitman	H
1850s—setting the poetic tradition in America	*The Poetry of Walt Whitman*	Walt Whitman	H
1850s—California gold rush	*Captain Bayley's Heir: A Tale of the California Gold Mines*	G. A. Henty	M H
1850s—California gold rush	*Captain Bayley's Heir: A Tale of the California Gold Mines* (unabridged audio book)	Jim Hodges http://jimhodgesaudiobooks.com	M H
mid-1850s—medical missionary to Africa	*Stanley and Livingstone: Story of Dr. David Livingstone*	1939 film starring Spencer Tracy	M H
1856—Maine	*Keep the Lights Burning, Abbie*	Peter and Connie Roop	E
1856—French impressionistic controversial novel	*Madame Bovary*	Gustave Flaubert	H
1857—portrayal of John Brown's raid	*Santa Fe Trail*	1940—film starring Ronald Reagan	M H

Ah, God! What trances of torments does that man endure who is consumed with one unachieved revengeful desire. He sleeps with clenched hands, and wakes with his own bloody nails in his palms .... When this hell in himself yawned in him, a wild cry would be heard through the ship, and with glaring eyes Ahab would burst from his state room, as though escaping from a bed that was on fire.

—Herman Melville, *Moby Dick*

Description or Time Period	Title	Author	Level
1858–1915—VA, WV, AL, GA, Washington, D.C.	*Up from Slavery* (autobiography of a slave)	Booker Taliaferro Washington	H
1858–1919	*Carry a Big Stick: The Uncommon Heroism of Theodore Roosevelt*	George Grant	M H
1858—life of George Armstrong Custer	*They Died With Their Boots On*	1941 film starring Errol Flynn	E M H
1859—English naturalist publishes the theory of evolution by natural selection.	*The Origin of Species* *(Compact Classics: Vol. I/5-K1)*	Charles Darwin	H
1859–1919—United States	*Bully for You, Teddy Roosevelt*	Jean Fritz	E M H
1858–1919—naturalist, hunter, author, soldier, 26th U.S. president	*Autobiography*	Theodore Roosevelt	H
1859–1865—American President	*Abraham Lincoln: Speeches and Writings 1859–1865*	Abraham Lincoln	H
early years as a young attorney	*Young Mr. Lincoln*	1939 film starring Henry Fonda	E M H
mid-1800s—New England gothic mystery	*The House of the Seven Gables* *(Compact Classics: Vol. III/p. 145)*	Nathaniel Hawthorne	H
1859–1930—Britain	*The Adventures of Sherlock Holmes* *(Compact Classics: Vol. III/p. 35)*	Sir Arthur Conan Doyle	M H
1859–1930—Edinburgh, Scotland	*The Adventures and Memoirs of Sherlock Holmes*	Sir Arthur Conan Doyle	M H
1859–1930—Britain and Scotland	*Sherlock Holmes for Children* (audio storytelling recording)	Jim Weiss http://greathall.com	E M
1884—murder mystery at a mansion near London	*The Hound of the Baskervilles* (based on the book by Sir Arthur Conan Doyle)	1939 film starring Basil Rathbone	H
1859—British philosopher; liberalism, empiricism, and utilitarianism; balancing constitutional order and individual freedom	*On Liberty* *(Compact Classics: Vol. II/p. 397)*	John Stuart Mill	H
mid-19th century—psychological fiction	*Crime and Punishment* *(Compact Classics: Vol. II/p. 189)*	Fyodor Dostoevsky	H
mid-1800s—New England	*Little Women (Compact Classics: Vol. I/5-J4)*	Louisa May Alcott	M H
mid-19th century—Concord, Massachusetts	*Little Women* (book by Louisa May Alcott)	1944 film with Katharine Hepburn	M H
1860—Missouri to California	*Riding the Pony Express*	Clyde Robert Bulla	E
1860–1861—Missouri to California	*The Pony Express—A Photographic History*	Bill and Jan Moeller	E

But, of old, there was One whose suffering changed an instrument of torture, degradation and shame, into a symbol of glory, honor, and immortal life; and, where His spirit is, neither degrading stripes, nor blood, nor insults, can make the Christian's last struggle less than glorious.

—Harriet Beecher Stowe, *Uncle Tom's Cabin*

Description or Time Period	Title	Author	Level
1860—St. Joseph, MO to Sacramento, CA	*Buffalo Bill and the Pony Express*	Eleanor Coerr	E
1860s—fictitious telling of the Pony Express	*Pony Express*	1953 film starring Charlton Heston	E M H
1860—Kansas territory, Pony Express	*Buffalo Bill*	Ingri and Edgar Parin D'Aulaire	E
1861–1865—major battles; Lee, Stuart, and Jackson	*With Lee in Virginia: A Tale of the Civil War*	G. A. Henty	M H
1861–1865—major battles with Lee, Stuart, and Jackson	*With Lee in Virginia: A Tale of the Civil War* (unabridged audio recording)	Jim Hodges http://jimhodgesaudiobooks.com	E M H
1860—England	*Peter Pan*	J. M. Barrie	M H
1860—poverty and ignorance in France	*Les Miserables*	Victor Hugo	H
1860—poverty and ignorance in France	*Les Miserables* (based on the book by Victor Hugo)	1947 film starring Michael Rennie	H
1860s—the story of Florence Nightingale	*The White Angel*	1936 film starring Kay Francis	M H
1861—English storyteller examines the human experience.	*Great Expectations*	Charles Dickens	H
1861–1865—American Civil War	*DK Visual Dictionary of the Civil War*	John Stanchak	E M H
1861–1865—gripping nine-part documentary; PBS mini-series detailing the Civil War; pictures; songs of the period; stories from Civil War historian Shelby Foote and others	*The Civil War* (Episodes One through Nine)	film by Ken Burns (1990) featuring Jason Robards, Morgan Freeman, and Sam Waterston	M H
biographies, battles, tactics, and weapons	*The Civil War Journal*	series by The History Channel	M H
1809–1865—American President	*Abraham Lincoln and the Heart of America* (audio recording)	Jim Weiss http://greathall.com	E M
1861–1863—story of Stonewall Jackson	*Gods and Generals*	2003 film starring Jeff Daniels	H
1861–1865—Kansas	*Rifles for Watie*	Harold Keith	M H
1861–1865—Civil War coming of age story	*Across Five Aprils*	Irene Hunt	M
1861–1865—War Between the States; chronological telling of battles	*With Lee in Virginia*	G. A. Henty	M
1807–1870—Virginia	*Call of Duty: The Sterling Nobility of Robert E. Lee*	J. Steven Wilkins	H
1861–post American Civil War	*Gone with the Wind*	Margaret Mitchell	H
1862—battle of the ironclads	*The Story of the Monitor and the Merrimac*	R. Conrad Stein	M H

We here highly resolve that these dead shall not have died in vain; that this nation, under God, shall have a new birth of freedom; and that the government of the people, by the people, for the people, shall not perish from the earth.

—Abraham Lincoln, "The Gettysburg Address," November 19, 1863, dedication of the first national military cemetery in the United States

Description or Time Period	Title	Author	Level
1860s—British governess serves in the royal court of Siam (Thailand).	*Anna and the King of Siam* (musical version: *The King and I*)	Margaret Landon	E M H
1862–1910—Greensboro, NC	*The Short Stories of O. Henry* *(Compact Classics: Vol. II/p. 73)*	William Sydney Porter	M H
1862–1910—Greensboro, NC	*O. Henry's Full House* (including "The Ransom of Red Chief")	1952 film version of five stories	H
1863–1947—Michigan; biography of a pioneer of modern manufacturing	*Henry Ford: The Wayward Capitalist* *(Compact Classics: Vol. III/p. 389)*	Carol Gelderman	M H
1863—American Civil War	*The Red Badge of Courage* *(Compact Classics: Vol. II/p. 137)*	Stephen Crane	M H
1863—American Civil War	*Lincoln—The Pivotal Year (1863)*	Jason Robards, narrator	M H
1863—Pennsylvania battlefield	"The Gettysburg Address"	Abraham Lincoln	E M H
1863—The Battle of Gettysburg	*The Killer Angels*	Michael Shaara	H
1863—recreation of the Battle of Gettysburg	*Gettysburg* (based on the book *The Killer Angels*)	1993 film starring Sam Elliott	H
1863—Gettysburg, PA	*Just a Few Words, Mr. Lincoln: The Story of the Gettysburg Address*	Jean Fritz	E
1863—Gettysburg, PA	*Slopes of War: A Novel of Gettysburg*	Norah A. Perez	M H
1863—Washington, D.C.; White House	*The Emancipation Proclamation*	Abraham Lincoln	E M H
1863—Civil War—Col. Robert Gould Shaw leads the all-black volunteer 54th Massachusetts Regiment.	*Glory*	1989 film starring Matthew Broderick and Denzel Washington	H
1863–1869—Transcontinental RR	*Union Pacific*	1939 film starring Barbara Stanwyck	M H
1860s—attempts to stop the last leg of the Westward expansion	*Western Union*	1941 film starring Randolph Scott	M H
1864–1943—American scientist, botanist, and inventor; alternate uses for peanuts, soybeans, and other crops	*George Washington Carver: Man's Slave Becomes God's Scientist*	David Collins	E M
1864—Wisconsin (based on a true story)	*Caddie Woodlawn*	Carol Ryrie Brink	E M

Jean Valjean was trembling in every limb. He took the two candlesticks mechanically ... Jean Valjean felt like a man who is just about to faint. The archbishop approached him, and said, in a low voice: "Forget not, never forget that you have promised me to use this silver to become an honest man." He continued solemnly: "Jean Valjean, my brother: you belong no longer to evil, but to good. It is your soul that I am buying for you. I withdraw it from dark thoughts and from the spirit of perdition, and I give it to God!"

—Victor Hugo, *Les Miserables*

Description or Time Period	Title	Author	Level
1864—autobiography; soul drawn to God	*The Justification of His Own Life*	John Henry Newman	H
Civil War spy	*Behind Rebel Lines*	Seymour Reit	H
American Civil War	*The Perilous Road*	William O. Steele	M
Mexico—volcano eruption; true story	*Hill of Fire*	Thomas P. Lewis	E
1860s—America	*Grace's Letter to Lincoln*	Peter Roop	E
1865—Washington, D.C.	*Lincoln—Now He Belongs to the Ages*	narrator: Jason Robards	M H
1865—metaphor; death of Abraham Lincoln	"O Captain! My Captain!"	Walt Whitman	H
1865—presidency of Andrew Johnson	*Tennessee Johnson*	1942 film starring Lionel Barrymore	M H
1865–1897—representations of Twain's best fiction	*The Complete Short Stories of Mark Twain* (Compact Classics: Vol. II/p. 147)	Mark Twain	M H
1865–1936—England	*Rudyard Kipling (Compact Classics: Vol. II/p. 261)*	biography	E M
1865–1890—post-Civil War America	*A History of US (7) Reconstructing America*	Joy Hakim	M H
post-Civil War—GA; textile workers	*Turn Homeward, Hannalee*	Patricia Beatty	E M H
post-Civil War—black family moves West	*Wagon Wheels*	Barbara Brenner	E
post-Civil War—Shenandoah Valley	*Shades of Gray*	Carolyn Reeder and Tim O'Brien	M H
post-Civil War—Brothers return from the war to find family and friends held hostage.	*The Shadow Riders* (based on the book by Louis L'Amour)	1982 film starring Tom Selleck and Sam Elliott	M H
Civil War era—Arizona; confederate prisoners; Indian attacks	*Escape from Ft. Bravo*	1953 film starring William Holden	H
post-Civil War—avoiding future conflict	*Great Sioux Uprising*	1953 film starring Jeff Chandler	M H
1860s—Texas–Mexican territory	*The Eagle and the Hawk*	1950 film starring John Payne	H
Civil War era—Westward expansion; gold rush	*How the West Was Won*	1962 film featuring all-star cast	E M H
late 1860s—frontier Texas hill country	*Old Yeller*	Fred Gipson	E M H
late 1860s—frontier Texas hill country	*Old Yeller* (based on the book by Fred Gipson)	1957 film starring Fess Parker	E M H

On Palm Sunday April 9, 1865, the war revisited Wilmer McLean. Confederate General Robert E. Lee was about to surrender to Lieutenant General Ulysses S. Grant. He sent a messenger to Appomattox Courthouse to find a place to meet. On April 8, 1865, the messenger knocked on McLean's door and requested the use of his home. Lee surrendered to Grant in the parlor of McLean's house, effectively ending the Civil War. Later, McLean is supposed to have said: "The war began in my front yard and ended in my front parlor."

—Ken Burns, *The Civil War*

Description or Time Period	Title	Author	Level
1860s—Texas-Mexican territory—U.S. law officers stop Maximilian from ruling Mexico.	*The Eagle and the Hawk*	1950 film starring Dennis O'Keefe	M H
post-Civil War Indian raids	*The Searchers*	1956 film starring John Wayne	M H
1860s—the American West	*In the Heart of the Rockies: A Story of Adventure in Colorado*	G. A. Henty	M H
1860s—the American West	*In the Heart of the Rockies: A Story of Adventure in Colorado* (unabridged audio book)	Jim Hodges http://jimhodgesaudiobooks.com	E M H
1860s—range wars in the Old West	*El Dorado*	1967 film starring John Wayne	M H
late 1860s—American wild west outlaws	*Jesse James*	1939 film starring Henry Fonda	M H
1860s—Oregon Trail	*Cassie's Journey: Going West in the 1860s*	Brett Harvey	E M
1860s—Oregon Trail	*The Wind Wagon*	Celia Lottridge	E M
late 1860s—realities of pioneer life	*The Days of Laura Ingalls Wilder*	T.L. Tedrow	E M
late 1860s—Mid-America	*The Little House Books*	Laura Ingalls Wilder	E
1867–1957—Mid-America	*A Little House Reader: A Collection of Writings by Laura Ingalls Wilder*	William Anderson, editor	E M H
homestead in Oregon	*Moccasin Trail*	Eloise Jarvis McGraw	E M
1860s—Transcontinental RR	*Dragon's Gate*	Laurence Yep	M
1866 publication	*The Strange Case of Dr. Jekyll and Mr. Hyde (Compact Classics: Vol. II/p. 163)*	Robert Louis Stevenson	H
1866—Russian exile publishes a work justifying murder for the higher purpose of doing good.	*Crime and Punishment (Compact Classics: Vol. II/p. 189)*	Fyodor Dostoyevsky	H
1867–1868—French oceanic scientist; Captain Nemo	*20,000 Leagues Under the Sea (Compact Classics: Vol. II/p. 119)*	Jules Verne	H
1867–1868—French oceanic scientist; Captain Nemo	*20,000 Leagues Under the Sea* (audio storytelling recording)	adapted and retold by Jim Weiss http://greathall.com	E M H
1867–1868—French oceanic scientist; Captain Nemo	*20,000 Leagues Under the Sea*	1954 film starring Kirk Douglas and James Mason	M H

O Captain! My Captain! rise up and hear the bells; Rise up—for you the flag is flung—for you the bugle trills, for you bouquets and ribbon'd wreaths—for you the shores a-crowding, for you they call, the swaying mass, their eager faces turning; Here Captain! dear father! This arm beneath your head! It is some dream that on the deck, you've fallen cold and dead.

—Walt Whitman, "O Captain, My Captain"

Description or Time Period	Title	Author	Level
1867–1912—Ohio; inventors of the first successful flying machine	*Wilbur and Orville Wright: "Fathers of Flight" (Compact Classics: Vol. I/4-D3)*	Biography: Inventors and Innovators	M H
1867–1948—Ohio, NC, France	*The Wright Brothers*	George Sullivan	E
1867—purchase of Alaska from Russia	*World in His Arms*	1952 film starring Gregory Peck	E M H
1868—Sweden; Oregon Trail	*The Long Way to a New Land*	Joan Sandin	E
1868—traveling across U.S.	*The Long Way Westward*	Joan Sandin	E
1868—New England	*Little Women (Compact Classics: Vol. I/5-J4)*	Louisa May Alcott	M H
1869–1948—India—peaceful revolution	*Gandhi: Peaceful Warrior*	Rae Bains	E
1869–1948—British colonial rule in India	*Gandhi*	1982 film starring Ben Kingsley	H
1869–1948—British colonial rule in India	*Mahatma Gandhi: "Peaceful, 'Great Soul'" (Compact Classics: Vol. I/4-E2)*	Biography: Leaders of the Spirit	M H
1869–1870—Meyer and Mendeleev	*The Mystery of the Periodic Table*	Benjamin D. Wiker	M H
1870–1917—America	*A History of US (8) An Age of Extremes*	Joy Hakim	M H
19th century—American South; sharecroppers	*Sounder (Compact Classics: Vol. II/p. 107)*	William H. Armstrong	M
1870–1914—connecting Atlantic and Pacific	*The Path Between the Seas: The Creation of the Panama Canal*	David McCullough	M H
1870s—treaty with Cochise; Apache Chief	*Broken Arrow*	1950 film starring James Stewart	M H
1870–1935	*World War I: The Rest of the Story and How It Affects You Today*	Richard Maybury	H
1874—most widely quoted English poet next to Shakespeare	*Poems*	Gerard Manley Hopkins	H
1874–1965—Britain	*Winston Churchill: Soldier, Statesman, Artist*	John B. Severance	E M H
1874–1965—Britain	*The Last Lion: Biography of Winston Churchill (Compact Classics: Vol. I/4-F3 and 4-F4)*	William Manchester	H
1874–1965—Britain	*Never Give In: The Extraordinary Character of Winston Churchill*	Stephen Mansfield	H

I heard the bells on Christmas Day, their old familiar carols play; And wild and sweet the words repeat of peace on earth, good will to men. And in despair I bowed my head: "There is no peace on earth," I said, "For hate is strong and mocks the song of peace on earth, good will to men." Then pealed the bells more loud and deep: "God is not dead, nor doth he sleep; The wrong shall fail, the right prevail, With peace on earth, good will to men."

—Henry Wadsworth Longfellow, 1863

Description or Time Period	Title	Author	Level
1874–1965—Britain	*Winston Churchill: "Britain's Courageous Bulldog" (Compact Classics: Vol. I/4–B1)*	Biography: Leaders in Crisis	M H
1875–1886—France to New York	*The Story of the Statue of Liberty*	Betsy Maestro	E
1875—Franco-American union	*Maiden Voyage—The Story of the Statue of Liberty*	Stephen Krensky	E M H
1875—classic Russian love story; tragedy	*Anna Karenina (Compact Classics: Vol. I/5-A4)*	Leo Tolstoy	H
1878—Kansas	*Wagon Wheels*	Barbara Brenner	E
1879—Cleveland, Ohio	*Moody's Great Sermons* (unabridged audio recording)	D. L. Moody http://jimhodgesaudiobooks.com	M H
1879—Transcontinental RR	*Across America on an Emigrant Train: Story of Robert Louis Stevenson*	Jim Murphy	M H
1879–1953—Russia; communism	*Stalin: Russia's Man of Steel* (illustrated biography)	Albert Marrin	M H
1879–1955—Ulm, Germany	*Albert Einstein: "Scientist-Mathematician-Genius" (Compact Classics: Vol. I/4-A5)*	Biography: Pioneers in Science	M H
1879–1955—Germany, Italy, Switzerland, U.S.	*Albert Einstein and the Theory of Relativity*	Robert Cwiklik	M H
1880s—true story	*The Big Balloon Race*	Eleanor Coerr	E
1880s—NYC to England	*Little Lord Fauntleroy* (story by Frances Hodgson Burnett)	1936 film featuring Mickey Rooney	E M H
1880s—India and England	*The Poetry of Rudyard Kipling (Compact Classics: Vol. II/p. 261)*	Rudyard Kipling	M H
1880s—relocation of Cheyenne tribe by army	*Cheyenne Autumn*	1964 film starring James Stewart	M H
1880s—American frontier; fictionalized telling of Billy the Kid	*Chisum*	1970 film starring John Wayne	H
1880—Idaho gold mining	*Bonanza Girl*	Patricia Beatty	M H
1880—rural New York	*Tuck Everlasting* (based on book by Natalie Babbitt)	2002 film starring Sissy Spacek	M H
1880–1968—the story of Helen Keller and her teacher Annie Sullivan	*The Miracle Worker*	1962 film starring Patty Duke	E M H
1880–1968—AL, MD, DC, PA, NY, and MS; young girl left deaf and blind by scarlet fever	*The Story of My Life: The Autobiography of Helen Keller (Compact Classics: Vol. III/p. 407)*	Helen Keller	M H
1880—Russian novel hopeful of a unified human race congealed by a universal belief in Christ	*The Brothers Karamazov* (based on the book by Fyodor Dostoyevsky)	1958 film starring Yul Brynner	H

Someone was drawing water and my teacher placed my hand under the spout. As the cool stream gushed over one hand, she [Annie Sullivan] spelled into the other the word water, first slowly, then rapidly. I stood still, my whole attention fixed upon the motions of her fingers. Suddenly, I felt somehow the mystery of language was revealed to me.

—Helen Keller, *The Story of My Life*

Description or Time Period	Title	Author	Level
1881—American storyteller sheds moral and psychological insight into humanity.	*The Portrait of a Lady*	Henry James	H
1883—Statue of Liberty; New York harbor	*The New Colossus*	Emma Lazarus	M H
1885–1945—biography of George Patton; leader of the American Third Army	*Patton, The Man Behind the Legend (Compact Classics: Vol. III/p. 409)*	Martin Blumenson	M H
1885—backwoods Missouri; social commentary on the many forms of moral enslavement; published in 1884	*The Adventures of Huckleberry Finn (Compact Classics: Vol. III/ p. 123)*	Mark Twain	M H
1885—published; search for ancient civilizations and mineral wealth in S. Africa	*King Solomon's Mines (Compact Classics: Vol. III/p. 143)*	Henry Rider Haggard	M H
1885—Dakota territory	*Dakota Dugout*	Ann Turner	E
1886 published	*Dr. Jekyll and Mr. Hyde* and *Weir of Hermiston*	Robert Louis Stevenson	H
1886—German philosopher criticizes the foundations of Western thought and morality.	*Beyond Good and Evil: Prelude to a Philosophy of the Future (Compact Classics: Vol. II/p. 403)*	Friedrich Nietzsche	H
1888—German philosopher; idolatry of self	*Twilight of the Idols*	Friedrich Nietzsche	H
1889—Wyoming; classic Western	*Shane (Compact Classics: Vol. II/p. 115)*	Jack Schaefer	M H
1890s—American Old West	*Buffalo Bill*	1944 film featuring an all-star cast	M H
1890s—America	*If You Lived 100 Years Ago*	Ann McGovern	E M
1890s—Victorian England	*The Importance of Being Earnest (Compact Classics: Vol. I/5-L1)*	Oscar Wilde	H
1890s—Victorian England	*The Importance of Being Earnest* (based on the book by Oscar Wilde)	1952 British film	M H
1890s—Britain	*Twelfth Night* (British film version of Shakespeare's play)	1996 film starring Ben Kingsley	H
1894—British colonial India	*The Jungle Book (Compact Classics: Vol. III/p. 3)*	Rudyard Kipling	M H
19th century English priest; sleuth	*The Amazing Adventures of Father Brown*	G.K. Chesterton	M H
1897–1976—Polynesian people	*Call It Courage*	Armstrong Sperry	E M H
1897—Alaska gold rush	*Call of the Wild (Compact Classics: Vol. I/5-E2)*	Jack London	M H
Yukon gold rush	*White Fang*	Jack London	M H

Give me your tired, your poor, your huddled masses yearning to breathe free, the wretched refuse of your teeming shore. Send these, the homeless, tempest-tossed, to me: I lift my lamp beside the golden door.

—Emma Lazarus

Description or Time Period	Title	Author	Level
late 1800s—rural Jackson, Wyoming; Indian sled racer	*Stone Fox (Compact Classics: Vol. II/p. 91)*	John Reynolds Gardiner	E M
late 19th century—Missouri sharecroppers	*Summer of the Monkeys*	Wilson Rawls	M H
late 1890s—Eastern Europe and England	*Dracula (Compact Classics: Vol. II/p. 165)*	Bram Stoker	H
1898—discovery of polonium and radium	*Something Out of Nothing: Marie Curie and Radium*	Carla Killough McClafferty	M H
1867–1934—Warsaw, Poland	*Marie Curie: "Lady of the Atomic Age" (Compact Classics: Vol. I/4-D2)*	biography	H
1898–1963—England	*Not a Tame Lion: The Spiritual Legacy of C.S. Lewis*	Terry W. Glaspey	H
1898–1963—fictional correspondence between hell and earth	*The Screwtape Letters (Compact Classics: Vol. II/p. 153)*	C.S. Lewis	H
1898–1963—fictional England	*The Chronicles of Narnia*	C.S. Lewis	M H
1898–1963	*That Hideous Strength*	C.S. Lewis	M H
1899—English fiction; colonial Congo	*Heart of Darkness* (based on the book by Joseph Conrad)	1993 film starring John Malkovich	H
1899—the honesty of human character	*Lord Jim (Compact Classics: Vol. III/p. 147)*	Joseph Conrad	H
20th century	*The Visual History of the Modern World*	Terry Burrows, general editor	E M H
early 20th century—New York	*All of a Kind Family*	Sydney Taylor	E M
1900—England	*A Treasury of Wisdom: Beatrix Potter* (audio storytelling recording)	Jim Weiss http://greathall.com	E M H
1900—England	*The Complete Tales of Beatrix Potter*	Beatrix Potter	E
early 1900s—Colorado ranch	*Little Britches series*	Ralph Moody	E M
early 1900s—Wisconsin	*Rascal*	Sterling North	E M
approx. 1900–Maine	*Miss Rumphius*	Barbara Cooney	E
approx. 1900—orphan; Prince Edward Island	*Anne of Green Gables*	L.M. Montgomery	M H
early 20th century—Ozark Mountains	*Where the Red Fern Grows (Compact Classics: Vol. III/p. 129)*	Wilson Rawls	E M

When Mr. Bilbo Baggins of Bag End announced that he would shortly be celebrating his eleventy-first birthday with a party of special magnificence, there was much talk and excitement in Hobbiton. Bilbo was very rich and very peculiar, and had been the wonder of the Shire for sixty years, ever since his remarkable disappearance and unexpected return .... It seemed unfair that anyone should possess (apparently) perpetual youth as well as (reputedly) inexhaustible wealth. "It will have to be paid for," they said. "It isn't natural, and trouble will come of it!"

—J.R.R. Tolkien, *The Fellowship of the Ring*

Description or Time Period	Title	Author	Level
early 20th century—north coast of Cuba	*The Old Man and the Sea* *(Compact Classics: Vol. I/5-D3)*	Ernest Hemingway	H
early 20th century—England	*The Secret Garden (Compact Classics: Vol. III/p. 9)*	Frances Hodgson Burnett	M H
early 20th century—Kansas; fantasy Land of Oz	*The Wonderful Wizard of Oz* *(Compact Classics: Vol. III/p. 11)*	L. Frank Baum	M
early 20th century—Kansas; fantasy Land of Oz	*The Wonderful Wizard of Oz* (based on the book by L. Frank Baum)	1939 film starring Judy Garland	E M H
early 20th century—Indiana farm	*Laddie: A True Blue Story*	Gene Stratton-Porter	E M H
early 1900s—England; early science fiction	*The War of the Worlds* *(Compact Classics: Vol. II/p. 171)*	H. G. Wells	H
early 20th century—China	*Little Pear*	Eleanor Frances Lattimore	E M
early 1900s—United States	*Mr. Popper's Penguins*	Richard and Florence Atwater	E
early 1900s—English countryside	*The Wind in the Willows* *(Compact Classics: Vol. III/p. 5)*	Kenneth Grahame	E
early 1900s—logging accident	*Lumber Camp Library*	Natalie Kinsey-Warnock	E M
1901–1909—Theodore Roosevelt	*The One Bad Thing about Father*	F. N. Monjo	E M
1901–1909—American president	*Carry a Big Stick: The Uncommon Heroism of Theodore Roosevelt*	George Grant	H
1902–1935—Washington, D.C.	*The Magnificent Yankee: The Story of Oliver Wendell Holmes, Jr.*	1950 film starring John Sturges	E M H
1903—Kitty Hawk, NC	*The Wright Brothers*	Quentin James Reynolds	E M
1903—Kitty Hawk, NC	*The Wright Brothers: How They Invented the Airplane*	Russell Freedman	E M
1867–1912; 1871–1948—Ohio	*Wilbur and Orville Wright: "Fathers of Flight"* *(Compact Classics: Vol. I/4-D3)*	biography	M H
1906—San Francisco earthquake	*Earthquake at Dawn*	Kristiana Gregory	M H

"It means," said Aslan, "that though the Witch knew the Deep Magic, there is a magic deeper still which she did not know. Her knowledge goes back only to the dawn of time. But if she could have looked a little further back, into the stillness and the darkness before Time dawned, she would have read there a different incantation. She would have known that when a willing victim who had committed no treachery was killed in a traitor's stead, the Table would crack and Death itself would start working backwards."

—C.S. Lewis, *The Lion, the Witch and the Wardrobe*

Description or Time Period	Title	Author	Level
1907—Victorian dialect; play by George Bernard Shaw	*Pygmalion (Compact Classics: Vol. II/p. 55)*	1938 film starring Leslie Howard	M H
musical based on GBS's *Pygmalion*	*My Fair Lady*	1964 musical with Audrey Hepburn	H
1908—Model T Ford	*We'll Race You Henry: A Story about Henry Ford*	Barbara Mitchell and Kathy Haubrich	E
written in 1910	*The Innocence of Father Brown*	G. K. Chesterton	H
1910–1997—Macedonia; India	*Teresa of Calcutta: Serving the Poorest of the Poor*	D. Jeanene Watson	E M
1910—Kansas; Maine	*Sarah, Plain and Tall*	Patricia MacLachlan	E M
1912—Kansas	*Skylark*	Patricia MacLachlan	E M
1912—story of the author's mother as a schoolteacher in the Smoky Mountains, TN	*Christy*	Catherine Marshall	M H
1912—Appalachia; Great Smoky Mountains	*Christy*	1994 series starring Kellie Martin and Tyne Daly	E M H
1912—North Atlantic	*Titanic: Lost and Found*	Judy Donnelly and Keith Kohler	E
1912—documentary on the sinking of RMS *Titanic* in the North Atlantic	*A Night to Remember*	1958 British film	M H
1910s—city girl in America	*"B" Is for Betsy*	Carolyn Haywood	E
1913–1962—New England	*The Poetry of Robert Frost (Compact Classics: Vol. II/p. 265)*	Robert Frost	H
1914—twelve short stories in the Tarzan series	*Jungle Tales of Tarzan*	Edgar Rice Burroughs	M H
1914—published; English couple marooned in jungles of West Africa; child raised by apes	*Tarzan of the Apes*	Edgar Rice Burroughs	M H
1914—one of forty such films made for the story of Tarzan	*Tarzan the Ape Man*	1932 film starring Johnny Weissmuller	M H
1914—America	*A History of US (9) War, Peace, and All That Jazz*	Joy Hakim	M H
1914–1918—Hungary; children managing alone	*The Singing Tree*	Kate Seredy	E M H
1914—Irish writer uses short stories to model innovative fictional methods.	*Dubliners*	James Joyce	H
early 20th century American author	*The Poetry of James Joyce (Compact Classics: Vol. II/p. 267)*	James Joyce	H

They seemed to be blinded by the light and kept blinking their eyes. One sat down on his little rear and started crying. The other one was waddling around and whimpering. I wanted so much to step over and pick them up. Several times I tried to move my feet, but they seemed to be nailed to the floor. I knew the pups were mine, all mine, yet I couldn't move. My heart started acting like a drunk grasshopper.

—Wilson Rawls, *Where the Red Fern Grows*

Description or Time Period	Title	Author	Level
early 20th century—first and biggest Ferris wheel	*The Great Wheel*	Robert Lawson	E M
early 20th century China—story of Gladys Aylward	*The Inn of the Sixth Happiness*	movie—Ingrid Bergman	E M H
early 20th century—headwaters of the Great Lakes	*Paddle-to-the-Sea*	Holling Clancy Holling	E M
early 20th century—survival in Catskill Mts.	*My Side of the Mountain*	Jean Craighead George	E M
prior to WW I and Russian revolution	*The House on Walenska Street*	Charlotte Herman	E M H
1917–1918—WW I; hospital	*After the Dancing Days*	Margaret I. Rostkowski	M H
WW I—Yanks coming to aid the Allies	*The Yanks Are Coming*	Albert Marrin	M H
WW I—perspective from home	*World War I—Letters from the Homefront*	Linda S. George	M
WW I—military leaders	*Leaders of World War I*	Stewart Ross	M H
WW I—technology in war	*The Technology of World War I*	Stewart Ross	M H
WW I—illustrated history of the American soldier, his uniform, and equipment	*Over There! The American Soldier in World War I*	Jonathan Gawne	M H
WW I—how the Great War devastated Europe	*DK Eyewitness Book: World War I: Life in the Trenches*	Simon Adams	E M H
WW I—perspective on war and history	*WW I: The Rest of the Story and How It Affects You Today*	Richard J. Maybury	M H
WW I—famous Western Front; German perspective	*All Quiet on the Western Front (Compact Classics: Vol. II/p. 207)*	Erich Maria Remarque	H
WW I—children care for soldiers and orphans	*The Singing Tree*	Kate Seredy	E M
WW I—Italy; Switzerland; reflects Hemingway's own life during WW I	*A Farewell to Arms (Compact Classics: Vol. I/5-A2)*	Ernest Hemingway	H

The yard was swarming with children waiting for the first glimpse of their new teacher. Most were flaxen-haired, skinny, too-pale, none dressed warmly enough for January .... As we got closer, I saw with a shock that many of them were barefooted. I knew that some had had to walk several miles in the snow. Suddenly I was painfully self-conscious about my foolish shoes. Their bare feet made me want to tuck my own feet out of sight to hide the tokens of my vanity.

—Catherine Marshall, *Christy*

No human mother could have shown more unselfish and sacrificing devotion than did this poor, wild brute for the little orphaned waif whom fate had thrown into her keeping.

—Edgar Rice Burroughs, *Tarzan of the Apes*

Description or Time Period	Title	Author	Level
WW I—Tennessee; Europe; biography of Alvin York; great American hero of WW I	*Sergeant York*	1941 film starring Gary Cooper and Walter Brennan	E M H
WW I—Tennessee, Europe; diaries of Alvin York, great American hero of WW I	*Sergeant York and the Great War*	Tom Skeyhill	H
WW I—Tennessee, Europe	*Sergeant York and the Great War* (retelling on DVD)	Richard Little Bear Wheeler	E M H
WW I—nurse executed for helping wounded soldiers escape; Belgium underground	*Nurse Edith Cavell*	1939 film starring Anna Neagle	H
WW I—Appalachian Mountains, NC	*The Year of the Perfect Christmas Tree*	Gloria Houston	E M
1918—autobiographical; baby raccoon	*Rascal*	Sterling North	E M H
1918—autobiographical story of the author's friendship with a baby raccoon	*Rascal* (based on the book by Sterling North)	1969 Disney adaptation starring Steve Forrest	E M H
1918–1945—Roaring Twenties; America	*A History of US (9) War, Peace and All That Jazz*	Joy Hakim	E M
1919—VA; prohibition	*Moonshiner's Son*	Carolyn Reeder	M H
1919—reprint of this classic	*The Aesop for Children* (126 fables)	Illustrated by Milo Winter	E M
the Great War—Appalachian Mountains, NC	*Littlejim*	Gloria Houston	M
1920—world-famous veterinarian who speaks the languages of the animals to better comprehend humans and the history of the world	*The Story of Dr. Dolittle: Being the History of His Peculiar Life at Home and Astonishing Adventures in Foreign Parts Never Before Printed*	Hugh Lofting	M
1920—world-famous veterinarian who speaks the languages of the animals	*Dr. Dolittle*	1967 musical starring Rex Harrison	E M H
1920—Danish immigrant; author	*Little Bear*	Else Homelund Minarik	E
1920s—introduction to Chinese culture	*Young Fu of the Upper Yangtze*	Elizabeth Foreman Lewis	E M H
1920s—New England after the Great War	*The Great Gatsby (Compact Classics: Vol. I/5-E3)*	F. Scott Fitzgerald	H
1920s—NJ; based on the true story of a family with twelve children; efficiency management	*Cheaper by the Dozen*	Frank B. Gilbreth and Ernestine Gilbreth Carey	E M H
1920s—NJ; based on the true story of a family with twelve children; efficiency management	*Cheaper by the Dozen* (based on the book by Frank B. Gilbreth)	1950 film starring Clifton Webb	M H

In Flanders fields the poppies blow between the crosses, row on row, that marked our place; and in the sky the larks, still bravely singing, fly scarce heard amid the guns below. We are the dead. Short days ago we lived, felt dawn, saw sunset glow, loved and were loved, and now we lie in Flanders fields.

—Dr. John McCrae, "In Flanders Fields"

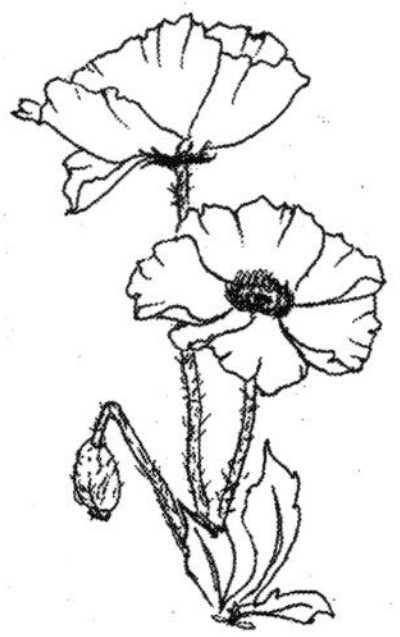

Description or Time Period	Title	Author	Level
1920s—Vermont; Shaker farm	*A Day No Pigs Would Die* *(Compact Classics: Vol. II/p. 99)*	Robert Newton Peck	H
1920s–1930s—Jim Crow laws	*Let the Circle Be Unbroken*	Mildred D. Taylor	H
1920s—British mystery series	*The Complete Stories*	Dorothy L. Sayers	M H
1920s—San Francisco; detective mystery	*The Maltese Falcon* *(Compact Classics: Vol. I/5-E1)*	Dashiell Hammett	H
1920s—British detective stories	*The Lord Peter Wimsey mystery series*	Dorothy L. Sayers	M H
1922—publication	*The Velveteen Rabbit*	Margery Williams	E
1924—Paris—Olympian	*Eric Liddell: Pure Gold*	David McCasland	H
1924—Paris Olympic games; story of Eric Liddell	*Chariots of Fire*	1981 film starring Ian Charleson	H
1924–2012—biography of medical missionary Dr. Robert Livingstone Foster	*Sword and Scalpel: A Surgeon's Story of Faith and Courage in Africa*	Lorry Lutz	M H
1925–1965—radical American extremist and former Islamic Black Muslim	*The Autobiography of Malcolm X* *(Compact Classics: Vol. I/4-F5)*	Malcolm X assisted by Alex Haley	H
1925—the spiritual journey of humanity and Western civilization	*The Everlasting Man*	G. K. Chesterton	H
1928—Scopes "Monkey Trial"; discussion of Darwin's theory of evolution	*Inherit the Wind* (from the play based on the Scopes "Monkey Trial")	1960 film starring Spencer Tracy	H
1925—Czechoslovakian agnostic writes of abandonment, estrangement, and alienation in our modern age (nihilism).	*The Trial*	Franz Kafka	H
1925—Alaska blizzard; diphtheria	*The Bravest Dog Ever: The True Story of Balto*	Natalie Standiford and Donald Cook	E
1925—true story of flying ace who trained pilots for bombing missions	*The Court-Marshal of Billy Mitchell*	1955 film starring Gary Cooper	H
mid-1920s Oregon	*Emily's Runaway Imagination*	Beverly Cleary	E M
1925–2002—People's Republic of China; hope during the cultural revolution	*Still Red*	Georgina Sam and David Wang	H

The mood in Paris (during the 1924 Olympic Games) itself was anything but somber. ... Pablo Picasso splashed his non-traditional inner self on canvas, while Igor Stravinsky electrified the world of symphony and ballet. Ernest Hemingway and F. Scott Fitzgerald were living the high life and writing of its emptiness .... The river of liberty and license rising in the United States during the Roaring Twenties had already breached its moral banks in the city by the Seine.

—David McCasland, *Eric Liddell: Pure Gold*

Description or Time Period	Title	Author	Level
1927—trans-Atlantic flight; Charles Lindbergh	*The Spirit of St. Louis*	1957 film starring James Stewart	E M H
1928—Netherlands	*God's Smuggler*	Brother Andrew	M H
1929–1968—Southeastern United States	*Martin Luther King, Jr.: "Modern-Day Author of American Civil Rights" (Compact Classics: Vol. I/4-E1)*	Biography: Leaders of the Spirit	M H
1929—Depression era	*Blue Willow*	Doris Gates	M H
1929—Great Depression; Irish immigrants	*Nothing to Fear*	Jackie French Koller	M H
retelling of Greek myth; sinfulness of selfishness; beauty of redemption	*Till We Have Faces*	C.S. Lewis	M H
Alaska Gold rush; Yukon territory	*The Call of the Wild (Compact Classics: Vol. I/5-E2)*	Jack London	E M
Alaska Gold rush; Yukon territory	*The Call of the Wild (based on the book by Jack London)*	1935 film starring Clark Gable	H
early 20th century—African American characters in rural South	*Their Eyes Were Watching God (Compact Classics: Vol. I/6-C5)*	Zora Neale Hurston	H
1930s—Oklahoma dustbowl	*Out of the Dust*	Karen Hesse	M H
1930—debut of mystery series for young girls	*Nancy Drew*	Carolyn Keene	M H
1930—debut of mystery series for young girls	*Nancy Drew* (based on the book series by Carolyn Keene)	1938 film version	M H
1930s—Southern sharecropping family	*Sounder (Compact Classics: Vol. II/p. 107)*	William H. Armstrong	M H
1930s—Southern sharecropping family	*Sounder* (based on the book by William H. Armstrong)	1972 film starring Cicely Tyson	M H
1930s—Oklahoma; California migrant workers; The Great Depression; dust bowl	*The Grapes of Wrath (Compact Classics: Vol. I/5-G1)*	John Steinbeck	H
1930s—Oklahoma; California migrant workers; The Great Depression; dust bowl	*The Grapes of Wrath* (based on book by John Steinbeck)	1940 film starring Henry Fonda	H
early 1930s—Yugoslavia; British upper class	*Murder on the Orient Express (Compact Classics: Vol. II/p. 167)*	Agatha Christie	M H

Bob [Dr. Foster] cannot stop challenging Christians to respond to the call to Africa's unreached people. He's seen their hopelessness and spiritual darkness. He's seen the wasted minds as no one has cared to teach them, and the weakened bodies without medicine or doctors. ... He longs that God in His sovereignty and mercy will break through, as he did in those Makua villages, with the Truth that will set them free.

—Lorry Lutz, *Sword and Scalpel: A Surgeon's Story of Faith and Courage in Africa*

Description or Time Period	Title	Author	Level
early 1930s—backwoods Florida	*Strawberry Girl*	Lois Lenski	E M
1930s—small-town boy scout troop	*Follow Me, Boys!*	1966 film starring Fred MacMurray	E M H
1930–1940—California; Norwegian immigrant family	*Mama's Bank Account* (made into film *I Remember Mama*)	Kathryn Forbes	M H
1931–1941—WW II—Japanese invasion of China to Japanese attack on Pearl Harbor	*Why We Fight*	Jim Hodges http://jimhodgesaudiobooks.com	M H
1932—published; story of the world we live in	*Van Loon's Geography*	Hendrik Willem van Loon	E M
1932—published in London; work of futuristic society	*Brave New World*	Aldous Huxley	H
1932—American master on par with Mark Twain	*The Short Stories of William Faulkner (Compact Classics: Vol. III/p. 27)*	William Faulkner	H
1933—discrimination in Mississippi	*Roll of Thunder, Hear My Cry (Compact Classics: Vol. III/p. 155)*	Mildred D. Taylor	M
20th century; pre-revolutionary China	*The Good Earth (Compact Classics: Vol. III/p. 157)*	Pearl S. Buck	M H
Depression Era—Maycomb, Alabama	*To Kill a Mockingbird (Compact Classics: Vol. I/5-M2)*	Harper Lee	H
Depression Era—Maycomb, Alabama	*To Kill a Mockingbird* (based on book by Harper Lee)	1962 film starring Gregory Peck	M H
introduction to worldviews	*7 Men Who Rule the World from the Grave* (Marx, Keynes, Wellhausen, Darwin, Dewey, Freud, and Kierkegaard)	Dave Breese	H
20th century's most evil figure	*Mein Kampf*	Adolf Hitler	H
1933—Germany; escape across Europe	*When Hitler Stole Pink Rabbit*	Judith Kerr	E M H
1933—how the Cross of Christ was used as a symbol of the Nazi agenda	*Hitler's Cross*	Erwin W. Lutzer	H
1933—Irish poet struggles with modern issues of materialism and abstract rationalism.	*The Poetry of William Butler Yeats (Compact Classics: Vol. II/p. 263)*	William Butler Yeats	H
1933–1947—Kentucky; championship thoroughbred	*Come On, Seabiscuit!* (unabridged reading by Jim Weiss)	Ralph Moody http://greathall.com	E M
1933—Washington, D.C.	*Nothing to Fear: FDR's Inner Circle and the Hundred Days That Created Modern America*	Adam Cohen	H

There ain't nobody gonna push me off my land! My grandpa took up this land 70 years ago, my pa was born here, we were all born on it. And some of us was killed on it! ... and some of us died on it. That's what make it our'n, bein' born on it, ... and workin' on it, ... and dyin' on it! And not no piece of paper with the writin' on it!

—John Steinbeck, *The Grapes of Wrath*

Description or Time Period	Title	Author	Level
mid-1930s—China; escape Nationalist forces of Chiang Kaishek; defining event in modern Chinese history	*China's Long March: 6,000 Miles of Danger*	Jean Fritz	M H
1930s—Yangtze River, China	*The Story About Ping*	Marjorie Flack	E
The Great Depression	*A Letter to Mrs. Roosevelt*	C. Coco De Young	E M
depression era	*It's a Wonderful Life*	1947 film starring James Stewart	E M H
early 20th century—U.S. Senate	*Mr. Smith Goes to Washington*	1939 film starring James Stewart	E M H
early 1930s—country vet; Yorkshire, England	*All Creatures Great and Small*	James Herriot	E M H
early 1930s—country vet; Yorkshire, England	*All Creatures Great and Small* (based on the book by James Herriot)	1974 U.S.—British film starring Simon Ward and Anthony Hopkins	E M H
1935–1941—lyric poetry speaks of redemption in a chaotic modern age	*Four Quartets*	T. S. Eliot	H
1937—published in England	*The Hobbit (Compact Classics: Vol. II/p. 87)*	J.R.R. Tolkien	M H
1937—rural Illinois	*A Year Down Under*	Richard Peck	M H
1937—Spanish Civil War	*For Whom the Bell Tolls (Compact Classics: Vol. I/5-A3)*	Ernest Hemingway	H
1939—backwoods Florida	*The Yearling*	Marjorie Rawlings	M H
1939—backwoods Florida	*The Yearling* (based on book by Marjorie Kinnan Rawlings)	1946 film starring Gregory Peck	E M H
1938—Jews in Hitler's Germany; escape to Switzerland	*Journey to America*	Sonia Levitin	H
1939—German-Austrian author	*Madeline*	Ludwig Bemelmans	E
reprint of 1938 classic	*Tales of a Korean Grandmother*	Frances Carpenter	E M H
1939—Speech therapist trains King George VI of England.	*The King's Speech* (based on a true story)	2010 film starring Colin Firth and Geoffrey Rush	H
1939–1941—North Atlantic sea battle	*Sink the Bismarck*	The History Channel	M H
1940—Dunkirk, France—evacuation	*The Snow Goose* (the Battle of Dunkirk)	Paul Gallico	M H
1940–1946—first black combat squadron	*The Tuskegee Airmen*	1995 starring Laurence Fishburne	H

I wanted you to see what real courage is, instead of getting the idea that courage is a man with a gun in his hand. It's when you know you're licked before you begin but you begin anyway and you see it through no matter what. You rarely win, but sometimes you do. Mrs. Dubose won, all ninety-eight pounds of her. According to her views, she died beholden to nothing and nobody. She was the bravest person I ever knew.

—Harper Lee, *To Kill a Mockingbird*

Description or Time Period	Title	Author	Level
WW II—unique perspective on history and war	*World War II: The Rest of the Story and How It Affects You Today*	Richard J. Maybury	M H
WW II—Austria; Nazi Germany; von Trapp family	*The Sound of Music*	Rodgers & Hammerstein	E M H
1941—every day battle between good and evil	*The Screwtape Letters*	C. S. Lewis	H
1941—Polish prisoner in Siberia, Russia	*The Endless Steppe*	Esther Hautzig	E M H
1941—events leading up to Pearl Harbor from Japanese and US viewpoints	*Tora! Tora! Tora!*	1970 film starring Jason Robards	H
Dec. 7, 1941—Pearl Harbor, Hawaii	*Pearl Harbor: Complete Live Radio Broadcast*	Jim Hodges http://jimhodgesaudiobooks.com	E M H
1941—Pearl Harbor, Hawaii	*Air Raid—Pearl Harbor!*	Theodore Taylor	M H
1942—life on an aircraft carrier; Battle of Midway	*Wing and a Prayer*	1944 film starring Don Ameche	H
1940s—WW II internment camp, Japan	*Farewell to Manzanar*	Jeanne Wakatsuki Houston and James D. Houston	M H
1942—Supreme Commander of the South Pacific Theatre of Operations	*MacArthur*	1977 film starring Gregory Peck	H
1940s—New York	*The Cricket in Times Square*	George Selden	M
Rural Tennessee; county fair	*Daniel's Duck*	Clyde Robert Bulla	E
1942 publication	*The Boxcar Children* series	Gertrude Chandler Warner	E M
1942—the story of Lou Gehrig	*The Pride of the Yankees*	1942 film starring Gary Cooper	H
1942—American novelist contributes to southern literary Renaissance	*Go Down, Moses*	William Faulkner	H
WW II—from the perspective of home	*The War*	2007 PBS series by Ken Burns	M H

For the second time in the lives of most of us we are at war. ... We have been forced into a conflict. For we are called, with our allies, to meet the challenge of a principle which, if it were to prevail, would be fatal to any civilized order in the world. ... For the sake of all that we ourselves hold dear, and of the world's order and peace, it is unthinkable that we should refuse to meet the challenge. ... There may be dark days ahead, and war can no longer be confined to the battlefield. But we can only do the right as we see the right and reverently commit our cause to God. If one and all we keep resolutely faithful to it, then, with God's help, we shall prevail.

—King George VI, September 1939

Description or Time Period	Title	Author	Level
1943—true story of patrol torpedo boat commanded by John F. Kennedy	*PT 109*	1963 film	M H
1943—Allies' campaign to capture German-occupied Greek Islands in the Battle of Leros	*The Guns of Navarone*	Alistair MacClean	H
1943—Allies' campaign to capture German-occupied Greek Islands in the Battle of Leros	*The Guns of Navarone* (based on the book by Alistair MacClean)	1961 film starring Gregory Peck and David Niven	H
1943—Denmark WW II; Nazi takeover	*Number the Stars*	Lois Lowry	M H
1943—series of radio lectures given to the people of Britain during WW II; apologetics	*Mere Christianity*	C. S. Lewis	H
1943—reflections on education	*The Abolition of Man*	C. S. Lewis	H
June 6, 1944—Allied invasion of Normandy, France	*D-Day: Complete Live Radio Broadcast*	Jim Hodges http://jimhodgesaudiobooks.com	M H
1944–1947—New York; end of WW II	*The Chosen (Compact Classics: Vol. I/6-D5)*	Chaim Potok	H
1945–post WW II—Europe	*A New Coat for Anna*	Harriet Zeifert	E
1945–2001—Cold War to War on Terror	*A History of US (10) All the People*	Joy Hakim	M H
1929–1945—Amsterdam; Auschwitz	*A Picture Book of Anne Frank*	David A. Adler	E
1942–1945—Amsterdam; Nazi occupation	*Anne Frank: The Diary of a Young Girl (Compact Classics: Vol. II/p. 231)*	Anne Frank	M H
WW II—Holland; Nazi Death camp; faith triumphs over evil in this true story	*The Hiding Place (Compact Classics: Vol. III/p. 201)*	Corrie ten Boom	M H
WW II—Gestapo captors	*Corrie ten Boom—Keeper of the Angels' Den*	Janet and Geoff Benge	E M H
1944—true story of how senior officials plotted to assassinate Hitler to save Germany	*Valkyrie*	2008 film starring Tom Cruise	H
1945—imprisonment and execution of German Lutheran pastor during WW II	*Letters and Papers from Prison*	Dietrich Bonhoeffer	H
1945—Germany	"New Year, 1945" poem	Dietrich Bonhoeffer	H
WW II—Nazi occupation Holland; Dutch family hides British pilot.	*The Winged Watchman*	Hilda Van Stockum	E M

Yesterday, December 7th, 1941—a date which will live in infamy—the United States of America was suddenly and deliberately attacked by naval and air forces of the Empire of Japan. ... With confidence in our armed forces, with the unbounding determination of our people, we will gain the inevitable triumph—so help us God.

—Franklin Delano Roosevelt, Declaration of War, 1941

Description or Time Period	Title	Author	Level
WW II—Eastern Europe; the nature of evil	*The Painted Bird (Compact Classics: Vol. I/6-B2)*	Jerzy Kosinski	H
escape from E. European concentration camp	*North to Freedom or I Am David*	Anne Holm	M H
rifle invented in prison; used extensively in WW II	*Carbine Williams*	1952 film starring James Stewart	M H
WW II—bombing of London; fantasy; allegory	*The Lion, the Witch, and the Wardrobe (Compact Classics: Vol. II/p. 85)*	C. S. Lewis	E M H
Siberian prison camp during Stalin's rule	*One Day in the Life of Ivan Denisovich*	Aleksandr Solzhenitsyn	M H
WW II—Chinese boy adopted by U.S. airmen	*The House of Sixty Fathers*	Meindert DeJong	E M H
details of the events after D-Day	*Citizen Soldiers*	Stephen Ambrose	H
WW II—home from POW camp	*Miracles on Maple Hill*	Virginia Sorensen	E M H
1945—backwoods Florida	*Strawberry Girl*	Lois Lenski	
1945—raising of the flag at Iwo Jima	*Flags of Our Fathers*	James Bradley	M H
1946—Japan; WW II; non-fictional documentary on the atom bomb	*Hiroshima (Compact Classics: Vol. I/6-A5)*	John Hersey	H
WW II prison camp; prisoners of war	*Stalag 17*	1953 film starring William Holden	H
Post-WW II—underground system of the Cold War; behind the iron curtain; arms race between the Soviet Union and the U.S.	*Torn Curtain*	1966 film by Alfred Hitchcock	H
Post-WW II—war for independent Israel	*Exodus*	1960 film starring Paul Newman	H
WW II	*A Bell for Adano*	John Hersey	H
1946—essay by French philosopher and political activist	*Existentialism and Human Emotions (Compact Classics: Vol. II/p. 423)*	Jean-Paul Sartre	H
1947—Chinese immigrant; NY	*In the Year of the Boar and Jackie Robinson*	Bette Bao Lord	E M
1948—Alaska; teacher from England	*The Year of Miss Agnes*	Kirkpatrick Hill	E
1948—Maine	*Blueberries for Sal*	Robert McCloskey	E
1950—India	*Teresa of Calcutta: Serving the Poorest of the Poor*	N. Jeanene Watson	M H
1950—French Jew; Third Reich	*Waiting for God*	Simone Weil	H
1910–1997—Mother Teresa	*My Life for the Poor: Mother Teresa of Calcutta (Compact Classics: Vol. I/4-F1)*	Jose Luis Gonzalez-Balado and Janet N. Playfoot	M H
1910–1997—Mother Teresa	*Something Beautiful for God*	Malcolm Muggeridge	H

Some of the pictures photographers took of what the Allies found when they entered the concentration camps were so horrible that they were never published. When all the soldiers killed were added in, the Second World War claimed over fifty million lives and destroyed some of the world's most beautiful cities.

—Corrie ten Boom, The *Hiding Place*

Description or Time Period	Title	Author	Level
1950s—Oxford; biography of C. S. Lewis	*Shadowlands*	1993 British film	M H
1950s—communist takeover of North Korea; Japanese occupation	*Year of Impossible Goodbyes*	Sook Nyul Choi	M H
1950–1953—Korean War	*Pork Chop Hill*	1959 film starring Gregory Peck	H
1950s—jungle island; plane crash; after a nuclear war	*The Lord of the Flies (Compact Classics: Vol. I/6-B5)*	William Golding	H
1950s—New York City gang	*Run Baby Run*	Nicky Cruz	H
1950s—New Jersey; small-town hermit befriends young boy	*Onion John*	Joseph Krumgold	M H
1951—Cuba	*The Old Man and the Sea (Compact Classics: Vol. I/5-D3)*	Ernest Hemingway	H
1952—mid-west Americana	*Charlotte's Web (Compact Classics: Vol. II/p. 93)*	E.B. White	E M
1952 publication	*The Biggest Bear*	Lynd Kendall Ward	E
1952–1953—historical documentary television series; Naval warfare during WW II	*Victory at Sea*	Jim Hodges http://jimhodgesaudiobooks.com	M H
1954—published; The Lord of the Rings—Vol. 1	*The Fellowship of the Ring*	J.R.R. Tolkien	M H
The Lord of the Rings trilogy	*The Fellowship of the Ring*	2001 film starring Elijah Wood, Sean Astin, and Ian McKellen	M H
1954—published; The Lord of the Rings—Vol. 2	*The Two Towers*	J.R.R. Tolkien	M H
The Lord of the Rings trilogy	*The Two Towers*	2002 film starring Elijah Wood, Sean Astin, and Ian McKellen	M H
1955—published; The Lord of the Rings—Vol. 3	*The Return of the King*	J.R.R. Tolkien	M H
The Lord of the Rings trilogy	*The Return of the King*	2003 film starring Elijah Wood, Sean Astin, and Ian McKellen	M H
1954–1973—Vietnam War	*Operation Dumbo Drop: Ho Chi Minh Trail*	1995 film starring Danny Glover	M H
1954—political courage facing adversity	*Profiles in Courage*	Senator John F. Kennedy	M H
1955—lessons on personal finance from stories	*The Richest Man in Babylon*	George S. Clason	H
1956—Ecuador; missionaries killed by Auca Indians	*Shadow of the Almighty: The Life and Testament of Jim Elliot* (1927–1956)	Elisabeth Elliot	M H
1956—Auca Indians of Ecuador	*Through Gates of Splendor*	Elisabeth Elliot	H
1956—Ecuador jungles; true story of Nate Saint	*The End of the Spear*	2005 film starring Chad Allen	M H
1956—Philadelphia, PA—Quito, Ecuador	*Nate Saint: On a Wing and a Prayer* (1923–1956)	Janet and Geoff Benge	E M H

An Iron Curtain has descended across the continent.

—Winston Churchill, 5 March 1946

Description or Time Period	Title	Author	Level
1957—WV coal mining town; true story	*October Sky*	1999 film starring Jake Gyllenhaal	M H
1959–1975—Vietnam War	*America and Vietnam: The Elephant and the Tiger*	Albert Marrin	M H
1960s—NY—gang and drug violence	*The Cross and the Switchblade*	David Wilkerson	H
1960s—Everglades	*Gentle Ben*	Walt Morey	M H
1962—New Guinea	*Peace Child*	Don Richardson	H
1962—Soviet concentration camp	*One Day in the Life of Ivan Denisovich*	Aleksandr I. Solzhenitsyn	H
1963—Lincoln Memorial; Washington, DC	*"I Have A Dream" (Compact Classics: Vol. III/p. 275)*	Martin Luther King, Jr.	H
1960s—New Guinea	*Torches of Joy: A Stone Age Tribe's Encounter with the Gospel*	John Dekker	M H
1960s—earth; various dimensions	*A Wrinkle in Time (Compact Classics: Vol. III/p. 7)*	Madeleine L'Engle	M
1960s—Jackson, Mississippi; Jim Crow laws; treatment of blacks from their perspective	*The Help*	Kathryn Stockett	H
1968—Vietnam; stomach-churning violence and language	*Fallen Angels*	Walter Dean Myers	H
late 1960s—Chinese cultural revolution	*Red Scarf Girl: A Memoir of the Cultural Revolution*	Ji-Li Jiang	M H
1968—New Testament truth relevant in the 20th century	*The God Who Is There*	Francis A. Schaeffer	H
1970—disabled craft and crew return to Earth	*Apollo 13*	1995 film starring Tom Hanks	H
1970s—biography of British Prime Minister	*The Iron Lady: A Biography of Margaret Thatcher (Compact Classics: Vol. III/p.417)*	Hugo Young	M H
1974—U.S. missionary	*Eternity in Their Hearts*	Don Richardson	M H
apartheid—Johannesburg, S. Africa	*Journey to Jo'burg*	Beverley Naidoo	E M H
1970s—Pre-teen deals with the death of a friend.	*Bridge to Terabithia*	Katherine Paterson	M
contemporary—home destroyed by fire	*A Chair for My Mother*	Vera B. Williams	E
contemporary	*The Best Christmas Pageant Ever*	Barbara Robinson	E M
contemporary Canadian wilderness	*Hatchet (Compact Classics: Vol. III/p. 133)*	Gary Paulsen	M
contemporary England—imaginative	*The Indian in the Cupboard*	Lynne Reid Banks	M
late 19th century—England; futuristic science fiction	*The Time Machine (Compact Classics: Vol. I/5-F3)*	Herbert George Wells	H
satirical allegory; Soviet totalitarianism	*Animal Farm (Compact Classics: Vol. II/p. 135)*	George Orwell	H

The hunger for love is much more difficult to remove than the hunger for bread.

—Mother Teresa

Description or Time Period	Title	Author	Level
from the fall of Rome to the Atomic Age; analysis of key moments, men, and ideas; influence on the condition and direction of our present culture	*How Should We Then Live? The Rise and Decline of Western Thought and Culture*	Francis A. Schaeffer	H
a book of Christian evidences	*Don't Check Your Brains at the Door*	Josh McDowell	M H
insight into spiritual warfare; prayer	*This Present Darkness*	Frank Peretti	H
NJ high school—true story of the principal who cleaned up the drugs, gangs, and test scores	*Lean on Me*	1989 film starring Morgan Freeman	H
1979—examination of financial practices; U.S. government	*How to Prosper During the Coming Bad Years (Compact Classics: Vol. I/ 2-C2)*	Howard J. Ruff	H
1980s history texts	*Lies My Teacher Told Me*	James W. Loewen	H
1982—Vietnamese culture	*The Land I Lost: Adventures of a Boy in Vietnam*	Quang Nhuong Huynh and Vo-Dihn Mai	E M H
1983—published; the value of human life has been replaced with quality of life; the result: abortion, infanticide, euthanasia, etc.	*Whatever Happened to the Human Race?*	Francis A. Schaeffer, C. Everett Koop, MD	H
futuristic London	*1984 (Compact Classics: Vol. I/5-G4)*	George Orwell	H
slavery, abortion, drunk driving, pollution, banking and credit, victims' rights	*Tools of Dominion: The Case Laws of Exodus*	Gary North	H
the abortion debate	*The Unaborted Socrates*	Peter Kreeft	H
denial of truth, meaning, and individual identity	*Postmodern Times*	Gene Edward Veith	H
cloning, drug abuse, social control through politics and the media	*Brave New World*	Aldous Huxley	H
inflation, stock market ... effects on economy	*The Money Mystery*	Richard J. Maybury	M H
economics—money, inflation, recession, wages	*Whatever Happened to Penny Candy?*	Richard J. Maybury	M H
introduction to business	*The Toothpaste Millionaire*	Jean Merrill	E M
present-day West Virginia	*Shiloh*	Phyllis Reynolds Naylor	E M
present-day Florida	*Because of Winn Dixie* (based on the book by Kate DiCamillo)	2005 film starring AnnaSophia Robb	M H
present-day California	*Nancy Drew* (based on series by Carolyn Keene)	2007 film starring Emma Roberts	M H
present day—effects of Darwinism	*Expelled*	2008 documentary by Ben Stein	H
modern U.S.—imaginative	*Holes*	Louis Sachar	E M

The real fire within the builders of America was faith—faith in a Provident God whose hand supported and guided them; faith in themselves as the children of God … faith in their country and its principles that proclaimed man's right to freedom and justice.

—Dwight David Eisenhower

Description or Time Period	Title	Author	Level
modern tall tale—near Philadelphia	*Maniac Magee*	Jerry Spinelli	M
science fiction—futuristic U.S.	*Fahrenheit 451 (Compact Classics: Vol. II/p. 179)*	Ray Bradbury	M H
1984—Cold War; submarine warfare	*The Hunt for Red October*	Tom Clancy	H
1985—North Atlantic	*Exploring the Titanic: How the Greatest Ship Ever Lost Was Found*	Robert D. Ballard	M H
1987—Alaskan Eskimos	*Water Sky*	Jean Craighead George	E M H
1987—United States	*Kingdoms in Conflict: An Insider's Challenging View of Politics, Power and the Pulpit*	Charles Colson	H
1989—off the coast of Costa Rica	*Jurassic Park (Compact Classics: Vol. II/p. 209)*	Michael Crichton	H
1989—published; the battle of ideas—the cause of evil, the meaning of history	*Answers for Difficult Days: Surviving the Storm of Secularism*	David Quine http://cornerstonecurriculum.com	H
1989	*The 7 Habits of Highly Effective People*	Stephen R. Covey	H
1991—English countryside	*Every Living Thing*	James Herriot	H
1991—remedies for the failure of modern secular education	*Recovering the Lost Tools of Learning: An Approach to Distinctively Christian Education*	Douglas Wilson	H
present-day Afghanistan; Taliban	*The Breadwinner*	Deborah Ellis	M H
1994—statistical portrait of behavioral trends	*The Index of Leading Cultural Indicators: Facts and Figures on the State of American Society*	William J. Bennett	H
1996—text on intelligent design	*Darwin's Black Box: The Biochemical Challenge to Evolution*	Michael J. Behe	H
impact of ideas in philosophy, science, art, literature, and film	*Saving Leonardo: A Call to Resist the Secular Assault on Mind, Morals, & Meaning*	Nancy Pearcey	H
the big picture of Western culture—a complete liberal education	*The Passion of the Western Mind: Understanding the Ideas That Have Shaped Our World View*	Richard Tarnas	H
political labels and their economic policies	*Are You Liberal? Conservative? Or Confused?*	Richard J. Maybury	M H
on learning how to think	*The Gift of Fire: With Wit and Daring, the Underground Grammarian Examines Why We Can't Think*	Richard Mitchell	H
1999—Littleton, CO—comfort and encouragement to friends and families after Columbine shooting	*This Is Your Time: Make Every Moment Count*	Michael W. Smith	H

Culture and the freedoms of people are fragile. Without a sufficient base, when such pressures come only time is needed—and often not a great deal of time—before there is a collapse.

—Francis A. Schaeffer, *How Should We Then Live? The Rise and Decline of Western Thought and Culture*

Description or Time Period	Title	Author	Level
terrorist attacks	The 9/11 Commission Report of the National Commission on Terrorist Attacks Upon the United States	National Commission on Terrorist Attacks	H
September 11, 2001—United Airlines Flight 93	*Let's Roll!: Ordinary People, Extraordinary Courage*	Lisa Beamer	H
2003—Hawaii; women's pro tour surfer returns to competition after shark attack	*Soul Surfer: A True Story of Faith, Family, and Fighting to Get Back on the Board*	Bethany Hamilton	M H
2004—revised and updated	*The Well-Trained Mind: A Guide to Classical Education at Home*	Susan Wise Bauer, Jessie Wise	H
present-day Hawaii—overcoming tragedy	*Soul Surfer*	2011 film starring AnnaSophia Robb	M H
2005—revised and updated; the onslaught of media and technology	*Amusing Ourselves to Death: Public Discourse in the Age of Show Business (Compact Classics: Vol. III/p. 303)*	Neil Postman	H
2006—worldwide pandemic of AIDS	*The Skeptic's Guide to the Global AIDS Crisis: Tough Questions Direct Answers*	Dale Hanson Bourke	H
2006—revised edition; the background, politics, philosophy, psychology and purposes of compulsory schooling	*The Underground History of American Education: An Intimate Investigation Into the Prison of Modern Schooling*	John Taylor Gatto	H
2006—revised and expanded edition	*A Thomas Jefferson Education: Teaching a Generation of Leaders for the Twenty-First Century*	Oliver DeMille	H
2006—published	*John Dewey & the Decline of American Education*	Henry T. Edmondson, III	H
2009—published	*The Coming Aristocracy: Education and the Future of Freedom*	Oliver DeMille	H
2015—published annually	*The World Almanac and Book of Facts*	World Almanac Books	M H
2015—published annually	*The World Almanac for Kids*	World Almanac Books	E

Freedom is a fragile thing and is never more than one generation away from extinction. It is not ours by inheritance; it must be fought for and defended constantly by each generation, for it comes only once to a people. Those who have known freedom and then lost it have never known it again.

—Ronald Reagan

Political ideology has a bloody and barbarous track record. ... Without some kind of transcendent truth, there is no way to stand against social and political evil. ... Lived out consistently, postmodernism leads to complicity with evil and injustice.

—Nancy Pearcey, *Saving Leonardo: A Call to Resist the Secular Assault on Mind, Morals, & Meaning*

Date Read	Title	Author

Date Read	Title	Author

Date Read	Title	Author

Date Read	Title	Author

Date Read	Title	Author

Appendix Contents

A Reader Response Journaling Sample:
The Magician's Nephew by C.S. Lewis

Here follows a sample of how to complete a Reader Response Journal. In order to read instructions for journaling about the literature you read, please refer back to pages 7–9.

Chapter 1—The Wrong Door

Vocabulary

study: room set apart for private reading, writing, or studying

holiday: cessation from work or duties for a period of time

cistern: reservoir, tank, or container for holding liquid

ginger-beer: carbonated ginger sweet drink

catch: anything that catches, as a latch on a door

cupboard: closet with shelves for dishes, cups, etc.

pantomime: actor who uses gestures to convey emotion without speaking

cunning: artfully subtle, shrewd, sly, or crafty

Sample Key Word Outline

I. London, Polly Plummer

1. meets, Digory, upset
2. D's, mother, ill,
3. D, lives, w/Aunt Letty, & Uncle Andrew
4. P & D, explore, attic, rafters
5. find, Uncle Andrew's, study
6. A, tall, thin, scientist
7. experiment, need, helpers
8. P, vanish, yellow, ring

Notable Quotes and Literary Devices

"Or he might have been a pirate, *like the man at the beginning of <u>Treasure Island</u>.*" (page 5) (allusion)

"If vacuum cleaners had been invented in those days Polly would have thought it was *the sound of a Hoover* being worked a long way off." (page 12) (allusion)

"The high-backed chair in front of the fire moved suddenly and there rose up out of it—*like a pantomime demon coming up out of a trapdoor*—the alarming form of Uncle Andrew." (page 13) (simile)

"Uncle Andrew was tall and very thin. He had a ... great tousled *mop of gray hair*." (page 13) (metaphor)

Samples and Definitions of Literary Devices

Alliteration– same initial letter or letter blend sounds which occur close together

"Tom joined the mob of skylarking scholars outside." – Mark Twain, *The Adventures of Tom Sawyer*

"In a moment all the heavy sorrow and misery which sleep had banished were upon him again, and he realized that he was no longer a *petted prince* in a *palace* with the adoring eyes of a nation upon him, but a *pauper*, an outcast, clothed in rags, *prisoner* in a den fit only for beasts, and consorting with beggars and thieves." – Mark Twain, *The Prince and the Pauper*

"The soldiers presented arms with their halberds, opened the gates, and presented again as the little *Prince* of *Poverty* passed in, in his fluttering rags, to join hands with the *Prince* of Limitless *Plenty*." – Mark Twain, *The Prince and the Pauper*

Allusion– reference to literature, historical events, culture, well-known ideas

"We were soon all in the water, Fritz with a harpoon, Ernest with a rod and line, and I myself armed, *like Neptune, with an iron trident*, or more properly speaking, perhaps, a pitchfork." – Johann D. Wyss, *The Swiss Family Robinson*

"Seeing this, I determined to make a raid upon them by torchlight, after the manner of *the colonists in Virginia*." – Johann D. Wyss, *The Swiss Family Robinson*

Assonance– same internal vowel sound in two or more words which occur close together

"The royal barge attended by its gorgeous fleet … was greeted from the banks with a continuous *hoarse roar* of cheers and the ceaseless flash and boom of artillery." – Mark Twain, *The Prince and the Pauper*

"In a little while the *measured tread* of military *men* was heard approaching, and the culprits entered the presence in charge of an undersheriff and escorted by a detail of the king's guard." – Mark Twain, *The Prince and the Pauper*

Foreshadowing– a hint at a future event in a plot

"Mistress Mary, quite contrary, how *does your garden grow*? With silver bells, and cockle shells, and marigolds all in a row." – Frances Hodgson Burnett, *The Secret Garden*

Imagery– word pictures that appeal to the senses, evoking feeling and mood

"A whole hour drifted by, the [school] *master sat nodding on his throne*, the air was *drowsy with the hum of study*." Mark Twain, *The Adventures of Tom Sawyer*

"And over walls and earth and trees and swinging sprays and tendrils *the fair green veil* of tender little leaves had crept, and in the grass under the trees and the gray urns in the alcoves and here and there everywhere were *touches or splashes of gold and purple and white* and the trees were *showing pink and snow* above his head and there were *fluttering wings* and *faint sweet pipes and humming* and *scents and scents*." – Frances Hodgson Burnett, *The Secret Garden*

Metaphor– comparison without *like* or *as*

"*The dreadful secret* of the murder was a chronic misery. It was a very *cancer* for permanency and pain." – Mark Twain, *The Adventures of Tom Sawyer*

"With this he dragged the frantic and struggling prince away and disappeared up a front court followed by a delighted and noisy *swarm of human vermin*." – Mark Twain, *The Prince and the Pauper*

Onomatopoeia– sound-effect words

"Countrymen, butchers, drovers, hawkers, boys, thieves, idlers, and vagabonds of every low grade, were mingled together in a mass; the *whistling* of drovers, the *barking* of dogs, the *bellowing* and *plunging* of oxen, the *bleating* of sheep, the *grunting* and *squeaking* of pigs, the cries of hawkers, the shouts, oaths, and quarreling on all sides; the *ringing* of bells and *roar* of voices, that issued from every public-house; the crowding, pushing, driving, beating, *whooping*, and *yelling*; the hideous and discordant din that resounded from every corner of the market; and the unwashed, unshaven, squalid, and dirty figures constantly running to and fro, and bursting in and out of the throng; rendered it a stunning and bewildering scene, which quite confounded the senses." – Charles Dickens, *Oliver Twist*

Personification – inanimate objects as lifelike or human

"The houses were of wood, with the second story projecting over the first, and the third *sticking its elbows* out beyond the second." – Mark Twain, *The Prince and the Pauper*

Simile– comparison with *like* or *as*

"Here Uncle Andrew rubbed his hands till his *knuckles cracked like fireworks*." – C.S. Lewis, *The Magician's Nephew*

"You know a noise sometimes brings things down – *like an avalanche in the Alps*." – C.S. Lewis, *The Magician's Nephew*

"To let a *sad thought* or a *bad* one get into your mind is *as dangerous as letting a scarlet fever germ* get into your body." – Frances Hodgson Burnett, *The Secret Garden*

Symbolism– objects, persons, pictures, things to represent an idea, virtue, or philosophy

"She must be less delicate before she begins lessons. Give her simple, healthy *food*. Let her *run wild* in the garden. Don't look after her too much. She needs *liberty* and *fresh air* and *romping* about." – Frances Hodgson Burnett, *The Secret Garden*

"When Fledge had quite finished his own excellent supper he lay down. The children came and sat one on each side of him leaning against his warm body, and when he had *spread his wing over* each they were really quite snug." – C.S. Lewis, *The Magician's Nephew*

Chapter 2—Digory and His Uncle

Vocabulary

fright: fear caused by sudden danger

vanish: disappear entirely

indignantly: anger due to unfairness

asylum: institution for caring for the mentally ill, orphans, or others requiring specialized care

bureau: low chest of drawers in a bedroom

adept: highly skilled, well-trained

chivalry: honorable, polite behavior

start: move suddenly

attend: pay attention to

Sample Key Word Outline

I. Uncle Andrew = magician

1. exp—ppl, vanish → "other places"
2. yellow, ring, (skin)
3. green r, → bring, back
4. A, trapped, Digory
5. D, agreed, → get, Polly
6. D, wore, 1 yellow r; took, 2 greens

Notable Quotes and Literary Devices

"My first task was of course to study the box itself. It was very ancient. And I knew enough even then to know that *it wasn't Greek, or Old Egyptian, or Babylonian, or Hittite, or Chinese*. It was older than any of those nations. Ah—that was a great day when I at last found out the truth. The box was Atlantean; *it came from the lost island of Atlantis*. That meant it was centuries older than any of the stone-age things they dig up in Europe. And it wasn't a rough, crude thing like them either. For in the very dawn of time *Atlantis was already a great city* with palaces and temples and learned men." (page 22) (allusion)

"Here Uncle Andrew rubbed his hands till his *knuckles cracked like fireworks*." (page 23) (simile)

Chapter 3—The Wood Between the Worlds

Vocabulary

horrid: extremely unpleasant or disagreeable

vague: unclear, indefinite

landmark: a prominent or conspicuous object which serves as a guide

quarrel: argument, disagreement

solemn: very serious, sad, formal

Sample Key Word Outline

I. Andrew, & study, vanished
   1. muddled, green, pool
   2. Digory, out → shore
   3. ⊘ wet, dozens, pools
   4. quiet: ⊘ birds, wind
   5. Polly, tree, guinea pig

Notable Quotes and Literary Devices

"This wood was very much alive ... Digory always said, 'It was a *rich* place: *as rich as plumcake.*'" (page 32) (simile)

"She was quite as brave as he about *some dangers (wasps*, for instance) but she was not so interested in finding out things nobody had ever heard of before; for Digory was the sort of person who wants to know everything, and *when he grew up he became the famous Professor Kirke* who comes into other books." (page 40) (allusion; foreshadowing)

"At first there were bright lights moving about in a black sky; Digory always thinks these were stars and even swears that he saw *Jupiter* quite close—close enough to see its moon. But almost at once there were rows and rows of roofs and chimney pots about them, and *they could see St. Paul's and knew they were looking at London* ... Then they could see Uncle Andrew, very vague and shadowy, but getting clearer and more solid-looking all the time ... But before he became quite real Polly shouted 'Change,' and they did change, and our *world faded away like a dream.*" (page 41) (allusion, allusion, simile)

Chapter 4—The Bell and the Hammer

Vocabulary

queer: strange, odd

eclipse: loss of power, success, popularity

rubble: decay; broken pieces from walls or buildings that have fallen

keen: strong ability to think clearly

threshold: bottom of a doorway or entry

vast: very great in size

pillar: large post that holds up a roof

deserted: abandoned, forsaken

avalanche: anything that falls or slides suddenly downward

flagstone: flat stone slab used especially for paving

ajar: partly open

enchantments: magical influence

Sample Key Word Outline

I. P & D → different, pool

1. arches, stone
2. chairs, people
3. waxed, figures, crowns
4. clothes, magically, ⊘ wear out
5. arch, bell, hammer
6. quarrel, P, reach → yellow, r
7. D, grabbed, P, struck, bell
8. louder, sweet, sound

Notable Quotes and Literary Devices

The notable quotes and literary devices, given on previous pages 93–97, can serve as examples for students' quotes and devices, which from here on can be chosen independently by students or with help from parent or teacher.

Possible Literary Devices might include alliteration, allusion, assonance, cliché, foreshadowing, imagery, metaphor, onomatopoeia, personification, simile, and symbolism, among others.

Chapter 5—The Deplorable Word

Vocabulary

stride: long step
masonry: bricks, stonework
peril: risk of injury, loss, destruction
ruin: decay, destruction
sulky: gloomy, dull, sullen
corridor: passageway
ebony: hard, heavy, durable black wood
rigid: stiff
terrace: series of levels rising one above another
dismal: dreary, cheerless, hopeless
contemptuous: disrespectful
incantation: spell, charm, sorcery, magic
potent: powerful, mighty, effective

Sample Key Word Outline

I. bell, awoke, Queen
    1. asked, D & P, broke, spell ?
    2. palace, breaking, Q P & D → left
    3. P, ⊘ trust/like, Q
    4. (Andrew's magic)
    5. escaped, iron, gates
    6. → Q's, magic
    7. Q = Jadis, 7' tall, beautiful
    8. Q, fought, sister → destroyed
    9. J, "deplorable word," survivor
    10. Q, wanted, D & P, take → world
    11. D & P, grabbed, rings, vanished

Chapter 6—The Beginning of Uncle Andrew's Troubles

Vocabulary

staleness: musty, stagnant, not fresh

stifled: suppressed, withheld

plunge: to forcibly penetrate, immerse, or submerge

conquest: to acquire by conquering

treachery: betrayal of trust; treason

ghastly: horrible, dreadful, frightful

grope: to search blindly

hansom: a horse-drawn covered vehicle with two wheels

Sample Key Word Outline

I. ↑ pool, wood, b/w, worlds

1. D & P, Witch, grabbed, P's, hair
2. discovery: D, touch P = magnet
3. P & D, rings, WW, grabbed, D's, ear
4. ↑ , Andrew's, study
5. WW: height, beauty, fierceness
6. Andrew = servant → WW

Chapter 7—What Happened at the Front Door

Vocabulary

cower: to crouch in fear or shame

minion: apprentice, subordinate, servile follower

lunatic: an insane, demented crazy person

rampage: violent, destructive, reckless behavior

mutton: the flesh of sheep

gallop: to ride at full speed

flogging: a beating with a whip or scourge

frock-coat: a man's knee-length coat

constable: a British police officer

bowler hat: a hard round hat

Sample Key Word Outline

I. slave! Andrew, chariot?

1. Letty: "Get out," WW
2. WW, threw, Letty, → room
3. "loose in London"
4. D, plan: touch, WW, rings
5. D, watch, Polly → bed
6. hope, cure, D's, mom
7. hansom
8. A, wrecked, "fierce horse"
9. police, & ppl, followed, horse
10. police, tried, help, WW
11. "dog"

Chapter 8—The Fight at the Lamp-post

Vocabulary

brandish: shake or wave as a weapon

nine-pin: ten pins without a head pin as in bowling pins

delirium: hallucination, delusion from fever or intoxication

vengeance: violent revenge intended to inflict trouble

Sample Key Word Outline

I. WW, angry, crowd, lamp-post

1. strong, attacked, "iron bar"
2. D, struggling, touch, WW (Jadis)
3. D + P + A + Cabby + Strawberry + Jadis
4. ↑ wood, J → pale, sickly
5. horse → drink, water
6. D & P, rings, ↓ new, pool
7. nothingness, ⊘ grass, trees
8. Cabby, thought, dead
9. Cabby + D + P, sing, hymn
10. A, whispered → D, WW heard, ⊘ attempt
11. beautiful, voice! wind
12. WW, hated, singing, STOP!
13. E, sky: valley, river, mtns
14. singer = lion
15. huge, shaggy, bright
16. D & P, threatened
17. leave: A + WW + Cabby + horse

Chapter 9—The Founding of Narnia

Vocabulary

nuisance: something offensive or annoying

sanatorium: hospital for chronic diseases

twopence: two British pennies

hedge: barrier of bushes, stone, etc.

veil: to cover or hide

Sample Key Word Outline

I. Lion's, song → beauty

1. grass, trees, flowers
2. Andrew, attempted, pick-pocket
3. Lamp-post, grew
4. WW, threw, iron bar → lion
5. WW, shrieked, & ran
6. A's, fantasy: everything, grows
7. millionaire, ⊘ cure, D's, mother
8. humps, appeared
9. dogs, frogs, panthers
10. birds, bee, butterflies
11. circle, animals, 2x, Aslan
12. A, touch, "chosen," noses
13. breathing → warm, breath
14. sang, again, "Narnia"

Chapter 10—The First Joke and Other Matters

Vocabulary

faun: deity representing men having the ears, horns, tail, and hind legs of a goat

jackdaw: glossy black bird in the crow family

repress: keep under control

muddled: jumbled; mentally confused

brute: crude person

sarcastic: scornful

Sample Key Word Outline

I. Lion's, voice, awake

1. hail →A, hear, obey
2. Strawb., chosen, "talking beast"
3. ⊘ dumb→ jokes, & justice
4. Narnia, est, keep, safe
5. P, D, Cabby → speak, 2, Aslan

Chapter 11—Digory and His Uncle Are Both in Trouble

Vocabulary

sagacious: smart, judicious, astute

revived: brought back to life

imitation: copy, simulation

curtsey: bow down

cockney: a squeamish, affected, or effeminate person

coronation: the act or ceremony of crowning a king, queen, or other sovereign

Sample Key Word Outline

I. animals, clothes=fur/feath.

1. ppl, ⊘ understand; communicate, w/animals
2. Andrew, fainted (2x)
3. A = the Neevil?
4. A = tree, plant →hole
5. A, withered, elephant, sprayed
6. A, revived, re-think, wickedness
7. Strawberry, & D, trotted → Aslan
8. D, asked A, help, 4 mother
9. evil, witch, Narnia
10. evil, entered, world
11. Mr & Mrs Cabby, king, queen
12. rule, judge, protect

Chapter 12—Strawberry's Adventure

Vocabulary

curvet: to leap as a horse from a rearing position, in which it springs up with the hind legs outstretched as the forelegs descend.

moorland: a tract of open, peaty, wasteland, often overgrown

dismount: to get off or alight from a horse, bicycle, etc.

descent: drop, plunge, downturn

upheaval: strong or violent change or disturbance

Sample Key Word Outline

I. Digory, quiet, uncomfortable
   1. A→D: undo, wrong, Narnia?
   2. ⊘, bargain, help, mom
   3. tears, A & D, know, grief
   4. A, plant, tree →Narnia
   5. repel, White Witch
   6. Lion's, kiss →D = courage
   7. D → mountains, cliffs, hills
   8. journey → bring, apple
   9. Strawberry →horse, "Fledge"
   10. D & P, ride, "Fledge"
   11. fly → green, places
   12. ↓ eat, rest, toffees (9-8=1)
   13. plant, 1, toffee → tree

Chapter 13—An Unexpected Meeting

Vocabulary

glaciers: an expansive mass of ice formed from falling snow accumulating over many years

alight: to dismount from a horse

saffron: a yellowish-orange color

pelt: to hurry

vault: to leap or spring

canter: to ride at an easy gallop

Sample Key Word Outline

I. sun ↑, toffee, tree!

1. baths, bfast = toffee + grass
2. 2nd, journey, heavenly, smell
3. "the place", golden, gate
4. D → alone, see, tree
5. 1, silver, apple → pocket
6. thirsty, hungry, taste?
7. warning, sign, shock!
8. Witch, stained, face
9. salty, white, face
10. WW, chased, D, tempted, w/info
11. WW, followed, spied
12. apple → heal, mother
13. D, kept, promise → Aslan
14. D, remembered, Aslan's, tears
15. D, apple → Aslan

Chapter 14—The Planting of the Tree

Vocabulary

bolt: run away, escape suddenly

coop: pen, cage

christened: named

half-sovereign: gold coin of the U.K. worth ten shillings

half-crown: former silver coin of Great Britain worth two shillings and sixpence

flagstaff: flagpole

Sample Key Word Outline

I. Well done!

1. D, seed → river, mud
2. coronation, Mr & Mrs Cabby
3. new, countenance, changed
4. sharp, quarreling, NY cabby →
5. courageous, kind
6. gold, silver, tree
7. muddy, Uncle Andrew
8. A → "coop" thistles, bees
9. fed, like, "pet"
10. Aslan, "breathe" → sleep
11. delicate, beautiful, crowns, x2
12. tree = joy, life
13. tree → WW = death, despair
14. apple, 4, mom = hope

Chapter 15—The End of This Story and the Beginning of All the Others

Vocabulary

housemaid: female domestic servant

banister: the rail of a staircase

trowel: hand tool with a scoop-like blade used for gardening

fortnight: two weeks, fourteen days and night

Sample Key Word Outline

I. ⊘ need, rings, w/Aslan

1. blink: P & D → wood, b/w worlds
2. ⊘ pool, Charn, dying
3. growing, like, her
4. WARNING: tyrant, nations
5. ⊘ joy, justice, mercy
6. COMMAND: bury, A's, rings
7. D & P, sensation, memory
8. golden, goodness = all, well
9. sad, afraid, remember
10. → London, lamppost, crowd
11. A - muddy, clothes
12. bottle, dressing-gown
13. P - get, rings
14. D - go, mother
15. "Apple of life"
16. bedroom, faded, dingy
17. smell, apple = "Heaven"
18. Mother, ate, slept
19. D, buried, core, & rings
20. Father, India, house
21. apple tree → "wardrobe"

The Story behind *Timeline of Classics*

Originally intended as a gift to my children, the document before you was not meant to be shared outside our family. Designed as a record-keeping tool for me, *Timeline of Classics* represents a portion of our seventeen-plus years of schooling at home. "The List" began on jumbo index cards the year I began building a high school transcript for our oldest child. Our project quickly made its way onto an expandable document—a portable timeline of sorts. The early copies became quite shopworn after having been highlighted, marked up, bent up, and spilled upon—solid evidence of their utility and countless trips to the library!

My own study of history was severely lacking. I had little more than a long trail of social studies and English tests, quizzes, and projects to show that I had done the hard work of studying history and literature. After having worked like a Trojan, I still had no idea how the Trojans fit into history. So, after spending years wrestling with historical characters and personalities from distant shores, tongues, and times, a logical solution emerged in, of all places, my filing system! In all of my 40+ years, chronology was the missing key in my own studies. Determined that this handicap would not pass to my children, I obsessively compiled our book list in chronological order. Necessity had truly invented The List!

Although it is not an exhaustive list of resources, *Timeline of Classics* presents some of the treasures uncovered during our search for classic literature, biographies, plays, and films portraying a given time period. Using this document along with an ongoing timeline project (such as Charlotte Mason's *Book of Centuries* or Sonlight's *Book of Time*) helps to create a mental framework on which to build and strengthen an understanding of who fits where in the story of mankind. William Ellery Channing stated: "In the best books, great men talk to us, give us their most precious thoughts, and pour their souls into ours." With that in mind, I have included a sampling of some of those thoughts along the pages of this resource.

Although I desire for my children to become lifelong learners, there is no way to experience everything on this list in a lifetime. (In my case, I have a lifetime of catching up to do!) Pick and choose wisely as your studies or interests dictate. Teaching your students to do this for themselves will benefit them richly. If one resource does not work out, then the good news is this: There is plenty to choose from! Suggested levels are given to include something for everyone (*E*=Elementary; *M*=Middle School; *H*=High School). These are approximations. Also, parents and teachers should exercise sound judgment regarding the use of movies to enrich learning. Previewing audio and video materials is always strongly recommended.

Even though *Timeline of Classics* was intended as a tool for students, anyone can use it. Because it was designed to be portable and user-friendly, please do not leave it on the shelf beside all the other books on recommended reading. The more contact students have with *Timeline of Classics*, the more they will learn from it. Make it your mission to add to the resources we discovered. And please, write on it. It would be gratifying for me to hear that your copy looks as bad as ours!

Institute for Excellence in Writing's Resources Related to Classic Literature

The Institute for Excellence in Writing (IEW) offers a wealth of information and resources for teaching with classics. Many of the products centered in great literature include IEW theme-based writing lessons, grammar and editing instruction, linguistic development through poetry, and literary analysis.

In addition to their collection of fine products, IEW has sponsored three Writing Educators' Symposiums. These gatherings resulted in a number of priceless workshops and sessions by a talented assembly of writers and educators. Please take an opportunity to invest in yourself as an educator. Enjoy! See the blue page for complete download instructions.

Talks

- *Nurturing Competent Communicators*—Andrew Pudewa
- *The Four Language Arts*—Andrew Pudewa
- *How to Cultivate Wisdom Through Writing*—Andrew Kern
- *Response to Literature*—Andrew Pudewa
- *Asking the Right Questions*—Adam Andrews

Articles

- "The End of Eloquence? Not on Our Watch!"—Andrew Pudewa
- "The Arts of Language"—Andrew Pudewa
- "One Myth and Two Truths: Nurturing Competent Communicators"—Andrew Pudewa

Compact Classics **and Other Helpful Finds**

If you own a copy of *Timeline of Classics*, you may be wondering why some titles have a notation underneath that says *Compact Classics*: Vol. I/5-H1, or some similar encryption. Many years ago I discovered *The Great American Bathroom Book*, a three-volume set originally titled *Compact Classics*. What a treasure! In just two pages, *Compact Classics* gives the reader an overview of the story, details on setting and character, and a brief commentary. For those of us who easily confuse the characters of Shakespeare or the plots of Dickens, these three little volumes are a lifesaver! And so, for your added convenience, all three volumes of *Compact Classics* have been indexed throughout *Timeline of Classics*. Put these on your wish list!

Reading aloud with our children is one of the single most important and enjoyable things we can ever do with them. While there is no substitute for marking the pages of a cherished favorite, modern technology makes classic literature fairly easy to obtain. Thankfully, busy families have convenient options. Many great works have been recorded as audio books and are readily available at your local library.

Master storyteller Jim Weiss (Greathall Productions) has worked to "bring to life for children the greatest stories from classical literature and history." Also, Jim Hodges Audio Books (Jim Hodges Productions) offer the largest collection of unabridged G.A. Henty historical novels available. Greathall Productions' and Jim Hodges Productions' products are for sale online. Websites at which you can freely download audio books in the public domain include *Librivox* and FreeClassicAudioBooks.com. Don't miss the golden voices of wonderfully talented narrators. (The auditory learners at my house really love this option!)

Also available on a number of electronic devices, e-books provide yet another alternative for both voracious and reluctant readers. So whether you prefer turning the pages of a book, listening to an audio version, or leafing your way through on a touch screen, find a way to fill your soul with classics!

Institute for Excellence in Writing
Listen. Speak. Read. Write. Think!

info@IEW.com • 800.856.5815

The Colloquium Environment

by Andrew Pudewa

(This article first appeared in the September 2012 issue of The Old Schoolhouse Magazine®.)

For the past ten years, I have always held a regularly scheduled colloquium for my teenage children and a small group of their friends. Unlike the terms "literature class" or "book club," *colloquium* carries no baggage, no connotations, few expectations. It doesn't imply that I will "teach" or that the students will do any particular type of "work"—a context that often attracts and rarely threatens.

In my early years I took some training in "Socratic" teaching, a methodology of focusing primarily on asking questions to help students discover answers for themselves (as opposed to the more common method of giving them answers to questions they would later be asked). Although this training occurred in the context of mathematics instruction, the basic approach carried over into all my teaching: math, music, writing, and especially literature.

During our colloquium sessions (a term from the Latin, *col-* 'together' + *loqui* 'to speak'), students meet and discuss great books. My role is that of facilitator, not instructor. To accomplish this, I must do a few things: (1) Set a projected schedule for readings and meetings; (2) Find the time to read the books I ask them to read; (3) Pencil out a few questions to start a discussion each week; and (4) Discipline myself not to dominate the conversation, inadvertently changing the conversation into a lecture. That's about it. So why have I found this to be such a good investment of time and effort? Many reasons.

First, a colloquium allows students to practice—in a formal way—the first two of the four language arts: listening and speaking. Yes, young people are listening and speaking all day, but the colloquium environment requires they do so in a focused and purposeful manner. To meaningfully contribute to a conversation, students must listen carefully and consider whether what they intend to say makes sense in the context of what has already been said. They are encouraged to speak in complete, grammatically correct sentences. The formality refines conversational skills.

In addition, the structured environment promotes a positive social atmosphere and positive peer pressure. Often, an assertive student with a tendency to dominate conversations will be put in his place by his peers. Likewise, a quiet, reticent student will often be drawn out by peers or by a

facilitator who asks him a direct question. My best groups have had a broad age range, from the sharp twelve-year-old to the high school graduate who wants to sit in with a younger sibling, and even a few parents (as long as they agree not to dominate the conversation).

Discussion promotes thinking, for what is thinking other than having a conversation with yourself? Good thinking is being able to ask good questions and using wisdom to judge the appropriateness of the answers you give yourself. By practicing asking questions of others, we refine our ability to ask questions of ourselves, thereby improving our thinking skills.

Mostly, this type of conversation helps to make literature relevant to the students. Great books address moral quandaries. Life is a moral question. Discussion facilitates necessary moral contemplation. Every teenager out there has three burning questions constantly at the core of his thinking: Who am I? Why am I here? And what am I going to do with my life? Of course, these questions imply that there are true answers and therefore that truth exists. Sadly, this is the one thing hard to address in public schools—a discussion of truth. Conversations about literature, however, require a context of truth, and consequently they become excellent opportunities to discuss worldviews, eternal realities, and what really matters.

Although I had a natural inclination towards this type of teaching, I found I was able to refine my approach over time with the help of a few aids. One breakthrough came when I attended Adam Andrews' very helpful seminar *Teaching the Classics*, and because I personally did the video editing for that product, I listened to the whole course many times over—some portions as many as a dozen times. I learned two things from that experience: One, hearing the same thing several times doesn't hurt me, and two, how to ask better questions—which is the whole purpose of the seminar. Additionally, I had my class as a laboratory wherein I could test various ideas.

However, one day after a class with a group of students ages 14 to 17, about six weeks into the book *Jane Eyre*, I found myself a bit frustrated and tired, feeling as though I hadn't successfully engaged the students. Reflecting on the experience I wanted for them but had failed to create, an obvious but previously unnoticed circumstance hit me powerfully. The class dynamic was stagnant because of the format; I was asking all the questions, the students were individually offering an idea or opinion, and then the exchange stopped. I wasn't creating the right environment; I wasn't truly facilitating a conversation. If that was going to happen, I somehow needed to decrease so they could increase; the discussion couldn't depend on me asking questions—that role had to expand to include them as well.

So the next week, as we got settled and after we went over the vocabulary words that the students noticed during their reading for the week, I began the discussion differently by making this statement: "So, someone ask a question about *Jane Eyre*." Silence. This was new territory for them. I remained silent. One asked, "What are you doing?" I responded, "Waiting for someone to ask a question about our book." More silence. Finally I think one of them got my point and ventured a question. I prompted another student to answer the question, "Diane, what do you say to that?" And I will admit that it was slow going for a while, with more than one moment of uncomfortable silence, but I persisted, intuitively knowing I was on the right track.

After a few months the environment had entirely changed. I had little to do but the occasional prompting or redirecting to prevent the discussion from getting totally off track, but I must say it went places where my mind never could have taken it. I remember one class in particular. We were talking about the nature of love (So much of *Jane Eyre* is about different types of love.), and one young man mentioned that he had read *The Four Loves* by C. S. Lewis, so I invited him to explain those to us. This prompted the question from another student: "I wonder if there are four corresponding types of hate?" From there it was almost a free-for-all, and although not much specific to *Jane Eyre* was discussed, I believe it was one of the best—and possibly the most important—conversations we ever had.

But you don't have to be an expert to get started. Dive in and try. Get a small group of kids, get a book worth reading, schedule a time, and start talking. You'll be amazed at what the colloquium environment can do.

Acknowledgments

For my children, Michal, Jeb, Kace, and Matthew Ledbetter, who laughed and cried with me through a great many of these classics. I will always be fond of all the places we managed to read together: the boat, the car, the tree house, the lake, the tent, the hammocks, the command chair, and, of course, the couch. You are the best!

While I am indebted to many for their support of *Timeline of Classics*, I am sincerely grateful to

- my husband, Shane Ledbetter, whose love and support carried me through this effort
- my parents, Harold and Patsy McBane, who taught me the life lessons of hard work, common sense, and integrity in all things
- the countless friends, fellow teachers, and homeschool moms who believed in our guide and enthusiastically put it to use
- the students and teaching parents in my writing and literary analysis workshops who discussed and wrote about many works of classic literature
- Andrew Pudewa, Laura House, Julie Walker, Maria Gerber, and the staff of the Institute for Excellence in Writing, who patiently taught me to polish a rough stone
- my friend, Jill Hamilton, who first encouraged me to share *Timeline of Classics*

In addition to my family, I am earnestly indebted to many others who could never know of the impact they have made on my family and me. Ruth Beechick gave me the courage and the common sense to set aside textbooks and replace them with real books. Charlotte Mason taught me, among many beautiful lessons, the importance of "living books." John Taylor Gatto put into words much of what I witnessed, not only as a public school teacher, but sadly as a public school student. He courageously brought to light issues that I knew to be true. Mr. Gatto inspired me to "keep on keeping on" for the "Bianca's" I have known. My thanks go to Oliver DeMille for presenting a sensible alternative for implementing "the nurture and education" of our children. God help us all to catch the vision of leadership education. Adam Andrews taught me the not-so-scary nuts and bolts of literary analysis. Andrew Kern entrusted to me the ancient tools for discovering wisdom and virtue in literature. Thankfully, my life will never be the same because of these exemplary people.

Now that you have *Timeline of Classics* as a part of your educational toolbox, pile the kids into a favorite love seat, huddle around a crackling campfire, or crowd into a comfy hammock, and experience a gem from the bottomless treasure trove of classic literature. As you do, may God reveal more of Himself as you look deeply into the hearts and souls of men and women who have been the subjects of history for all time and the objects of His grace forever.

Gail Ledbetter